A Celebration of All Things *Lucy*

Inside the World of Television's First Great Sitcom

Elisabeth Edwards

AUTHORIZED BY CBS WORLDWIDE INC. AND THE ESTATES OF LUCILLE BALL AND DESI ARNAZ

RUNNING PRESS
PHILADELPHIA • LONDON

Books published by Running Press are available at special discounts for bulk purchases in the United States by corporations, institutions, and other organizations. For more information, please contact the Special Markets Department at the Perseus Books Group, 2300 Chestnut Street, Suite 200, Philadelphia, PA 19103, or call (800) 810-4145, ext. 5000, or e-mail special.markets@perseusbooks.com.

ISBN 978-0-7624-3976-8
Library of Congress Control Number: 2010943088

9 8 7 6 5 4 3 2 1
Digit on the right indicates the number of this printing

Designed by Melissa Gerber
Edited by Cindy De La Hoz
Typography: Adobe Garamond Pro, EdPs Roman, EdPs Bengbats, Justlefthand,
Sackers Gothic Light, and Savoye Plain

Running Press Book Publishers
2300 Chestnut Street
Philadelphia, PA 19103-4371

Visit us on the web!
www.runningpress.com

To Lucie Arnaz and Desi Arnaz, Jr.

Contents

Setting the Stage: America in the 1950s

In 1950s America, change was everywhere. World War II had ended and the Cold War between the U.S. and the Soviet Union and the Eastern Block countries had begun. The United States of America was the leader of the free world, ready to take the reins and rebuild war-torn Europe and Japan. The entire country seemed young, democratic, freethinking, energetic, and ready to roll. The returning soldiers were getting married in droves and starting families. Due to the GI Bill, veterans were given access to educations most could scarcely have envisioned a decade before. Jobs were plentiful and paid enough for average families to afford homes, automobiles, and vacations. Rising up the corporate ladder through ingenuity and hard work became something that every young man understood was a ticket to happiness and success. Into this new world stepped Lucille Ball and Desi Arnaz with their domestic television sitcom, *I Love Lucy*.

Much of the rapid change in 1950s America centered on the home. New appliances were being offered for families that had survived depression and war and were ready for a little extra convenience to go along with their peace. Modern appliances, once affordable to only the most wealthy Americans, were now readily available to anyone who could make a down payment followed by small weekly or monthly fees. The era of buying on credit had begun. Washing machines, dryers, dishwashers, ranges, garbage disposals, and even the first water-dispensing machines were being sold in department and appliance stores. The life of the American housewife was getting easier, and this fact was represented on *I Love Lucy* when Lucy demanded that Ricky buy her a clothes dryer after the baby was born. Of course, this turned into a whole episode about selling their old washing machine to the Mertzes.

I Love Lucy is a perfect microcosm for America in the 1950s in that it comprises so many of the aspects of life during that decade. For one thing, the roles of women were

1954 ARNAZ FAMILY PHOTO

slowly changing. Having been asked to work outside the home during the war, women had discovered some new facets of life, such as earning a wage and being able to do things other than wash and cook and clean. During the war, women had driven Jeeps, welded ships, and flown planes. *I Love Lucy* was no different. Its star was a woman, one of its writers was a woman, and Lucille Ball was co-owner of the company that produced it.

On the show itself some aspects of the expanding roles of women were shown. In the famous "Job Switching" episode from Season Two, Lucy and Ethel not only went out looking for work outside the home, but they switched

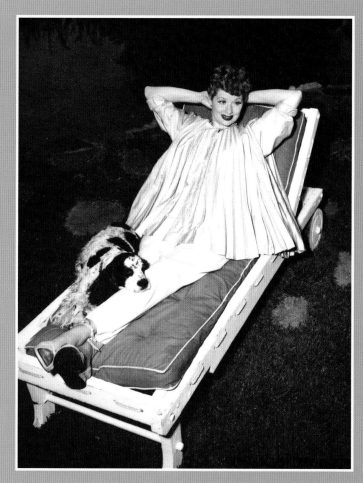

places with their husbands, who stayed home and cooked and cleaned. Lucy and Ethel both drove cars at various times, and partnered in a moneymaking business all by themselves more than once. The character of Ethel had a background of working in vaudeville, managing a diner, and she was co-owner of the apartment building they all lived in. And of course, Lucy and Ethel were always trying to get jobs in show biz, whether it be in a Hollywood film or in Ricky's club.

The funny thing about all this though, was that for all her bluster about getting ahead and being in the show, Lucy Ricardo, much like Lucille Ball, was not a feminist. Lucy once cries, "Oh, if only I had to do it all over, I'd just be happy to be Mrs. Ricky Ricardo." She and Ethel don't want to open a business because they want to prove to the world they can do it; they want to make money so they can buy more dresses and hats. Ricky still controls the household finances, and he keeps Lucy on an allowance. In one episode he asks Lucy to bring him *his* checkbook. She is always in some kind of financial trouble, making it look

like she is incapable of handling such matters and it would be best to leave it up to the men. Fred is the same way with Ethel, not allowing her to collect the rents or to have her own credit card.

The ladies (everyone called them "girls") had a foray into the world of equal rights in one episode, but it turns into a disaster—they still want Ricky and Fred to help them on with their coats, hold doors for them, pull out their chairs, let them order first, and pay for their meals. They want to be treated equally, just not *that* equally. And who could forget the time Ricky put his wife on a schedule that included specific times for her to take care of household chores, such as washing dishes, laundry, and cooking dinner. In other instances, the gals are caught up in the trap of competing with other women. Remember the times they try to glam themselves up for their hubbies? They don't go to charm school or dress in skin-tight gowns because they want to please themselves; they do it because they feel the need to compete with other women for the affections of their husbands.

Even when Lucy finally gets lucky with her acting abilities, she ends up turning down the offers in order to stay home with her family. In one of the very first episodes, she is offered a contract to take her "Professor" role on the road, but she turns it down in order to cook for Ricky, hand him his slippers, and be the mother of his children. Later, when she is offered a choice Hollywood job, she passes so that she can return to New York with her husband and child. She wouldn't dream of separating from her family, even for a chance at being internationally famous. There would be no daycare for Little Ricky, who only knew the loving arms of his parents, godparents, grandmothers, and Mrs. Trumble.

Lucy Ricardo was a PTA mom who always put the needs of her son and husband first. In that way, she was very much like other sitcom moms of her day, and very much like Lucille Ball herself. Lucille took her family with her wherever she went, and employed her brother, Fred, her cousin Cleo, Cleo's husband, Kenny Morgan, and her own second husband, Gary Morton, at various times. Lucie and Desi, Jr. were often cared for by Lucille's mother when Lucille herself wasn't available. She later became president of Desilu Studios, but she freely admitted she was never happy in the position of actually running the company. Desi had always been the businessman. Lucy kept on the trusted people to run the business aspect of the company while she continued to be a mother and wife, and to act in television shows.

Lucille always worked, but her desire to work came more from the feeling of never wanting to be poor again and from wanting to entertain. She never really gave a thought to breaking glass ceilings or carving out new paths for women. She had nothing against feminists; she just wasn't one herself. She was like most women of her generation—raised to be housewives and mothers, given a glimpse of the world outside that bubble, but not quite ready to change everything they had been taught and every cultural tenet of the day. Still, she set the bar for women who would follow her—Mary Tyler Moore, Carol Burnett, Betty White, Bea Arthur, Roseanne Barr, Debra Messing, Tina Fey, and Ellen DeGeneres can all tip their hats to Lucille Ball and Lucy Ricardo for getting it all started for the modern ladies of television comedy.

For all their wacky situations and schemes, Lucy and Ethel were perfect 1950s housewives. They could do it all in the home…

Lucy cooked.

They served tea.

Lucy cleaned.

Lucy dusted…

…then again, sometimes she gave new meaning to the chore of "dusting."

Lucy did laundry.

Another aspect of life that was changing rapidly in the 1950s was the way America traveled. Finally released from the challenges of gas rationing and able to afford inexpensive cars of their own, most middle-class Americans were making tracks. American families took vacations to the mountains and the beach, and as they moved away from their original families to other parts of the country, they would drive or fly home "to grandmother's house" for holidays.

The Ricardos and Mertzes went right along with this trend. In the fourth season they drove out to Hollywood together, after dismissing the choices of bus, rail, and air travel. They stopped along the way and saw the sights; they visited family and stayed in hotels (some of them better than others). They took the train home because they wouldn't need the car in New York, and then two seasons later Ricky bought a station wagon, a typical symbol of suburban living, when they moved to the country. In the fifth season they traveled by ship to Europe and toured the continent by train and bus. They flew across the Atlantic on a large jet, another representation of how the world was evolving after World War II.

Another change that was sweeping the nation was the move from the cities to the suburbs. All across the country, men who had left their ancestral homes and farms to go off to war were marrying, going to college, and finding jobs in fields they had never heard of. Many of them were finding these jobs in large cities, but since the cities were crowded and expensive, an easy solution was to move their families to the safety and quiet of the country, but still have easy commuting access to their jobs. Suburban sprawl spread throughout formerly quiet corners of America. Neighborhoods with look-alike houses sprang up almost overnight, inviting couples to stop paying rent in the crowded cities, but instead take out mortgages and move to the country, where they would find good schools, neighborhoods, churches, and social activities.

Once again, this societal change was revealed on *I Love Lucy* when first the Ricardos and then the Mertzes moved to the country. All of a sudden Lucy began to indicate that she had always wanted to get away from city life. She wanted her son to grow up with sunshine and grass and baseball and kite flying. So, being the loving husband that he was, Ricky took out a twenty-year mortgage and moved his family, including Fred the dog, to the clean air of Connecticut. He

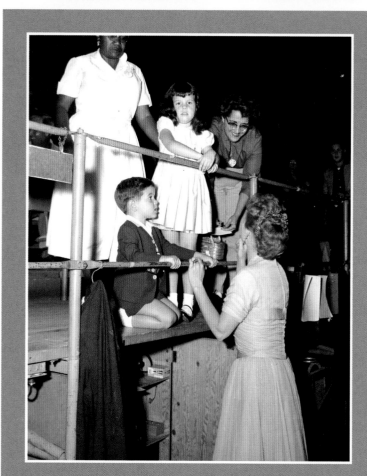

DESI JR. AND LUCIE ATTEND A FILMING OF *I LOVE LUCY*. THEIR CARETAKER, WILLIE MAE BARKER (BEHIND DESI) TOOK CARE OF THE ARNAZ CHILDREN WHILE THEIR PARENTS WORKED.

would still work in the city, and would commute by train. Not willing to be separated from their friends, the Mertzes would move too, in order to help Lucy and Ricky run their new egg business, which they had begun when they realized how expensive suburban life could really be.

As with the other changes in American culture, the life and structure of the American family was also undergoing constant shifts. While still quite a conservative nation, people saw the beginnings of movements that would impact the 1960s. Teenagers were becoming a force in American society. In a time when most of their parents had gone to high school and gotten jobs, 1950s teens had disposable income and disposable time. On *I Love Lucy* we saw teenagers Peggy and Arthur having crushes on the much older Ricardos, and Lucy talks about "that Elvis something or other," referring to original rock and roller Elvis Presley and the music that was sweeping the country and shaping an entire generation.

Other major events, such as Lucille Ball's real-life pregnancy, were not only discussed but spotlighted.

Although they couldn't say the word "pregnant," and although they moved the Ricardos' twin beds from being pushed together to pushed apart, Lucy Ricardo did have a baby with her husband. The storyline would not have happened if Lucille Ball had not actually been "in the family way," but that does not diminish the pioneering nature of what they did. The Arnazes received a handful of telegrams from angry viewers expressing their disgust at shining a light on the subject of marital relations but the few were juxtaposed against thousands of letters offering congratulations.

Episodes later, Lucy and Ethel are knocking on doors trying to find the woman who Lucy thinks is leading Ricky astray, and they are asked if they are taking polls for Alfred Kinsey, a biologist who was then putting together groundbreaking reports on the subject of human sexuality. Although these subjects seem quaintly tame to our modern sensibilities, in the time of *I Love Lucy* they were rather taboo subjects, ones that had not yet seen the light of day on television.

Other facets of American life, such as politics, were also referenced on the show. Among the presidents mentioned were Lincoln, Theodore Roosevelt, Truman, and Eisenhower. During a club election, Lucy calls for a caucus, and Ethel mentions that she would never have known to do such a thing had she not watched the recent nominating conventions on television. Although they never discussed voting in any national elections, the Ricardos and their pals, like most Americans of the day, were becoming more knowledgeable about and involved in political activities.

Of course, there were some holdovers from bygone days that helped with some of the plots on the show. In the 1950s, party lines were becoming obsolete, even though they had been the way many Americans used their phones, especially in apartment buildings and cities. Here's how they worked: Two or more customers are connected to the same line. The ring would occur on all phones simultaneously, but the rings would be different for each client so everyone could distinguish their calls from those of their neighbors. Of course, the usage of party lines by the writers was a wonderful way for the characters to either

LUCY AND LUCIE

hear gossip or to hinder the making or receiving of a call. Party lines were a perfect plot device, especially when they allowed eavesdropping. The 1959 film *Pillow Talk* (starring Doris Day and Rock Hudson) made wonderful use of the party line as a method of snooping.

Finally, although certainly not a new phenomenon in the 1950s, American ingenuity, can-do spirit, and ambition were alive and well, both in real life and on *I Love Lucy*. Like most American men of his day, Ricky is constantly trying to get ahead. Whether it's asking for a raise, buying the Tropicana and renaming it Club Babalu, going to Hollywood to make a picture, touring Europe with his band, or going into business for himself, Ricky is always looking for ways to improve his life and that of his family.

LUCY RICARDO MAY HAVE BEEN A STAY-AT-HOME MOM, BUT LUCILLE BALL WAS A WORKING MOTHER. THIS IS A TENDER MOMENT WITH HER KIDS BEFORE LEAVING THEM WITH THEIR CARETAKER.

THE QUEEN OF COMEDY, ALL MADE UP FOR "THE FREEZER"

He talks about sending Little Ricky to college, and Lucy wants her son to be a doctor. All of these ideas are typical of the post-war generation of Americans.

Fred Mertz is more of a holdover from past generations, especially those who suffered through the Depression. Fred is of retirement age, and mostly concerned with having enough money to survive, should things get bad again. He would earn money if he needed to, through acting or performing (or chicken farming), but Fred would be more interested in sitting back and watching it roll in through some investment or other scheme. Fred is as cheap as they come, but that would have been very understandable to the viewing audience that had lived through the 1930s and early '40s.

Lucy is also interested in making a buck, since she is usually in trouble with Ricky for buying too many hats or dresses. She goes into business as a babysitter, a salad dressing entrepreneur, and a dress shop owner. In order to give the appearance of being as financially well off as her former classmates, she is forced to take a job as a woman from Mars and climb the Empire State Building to terrify tourists and the city of New York. Along with her desire

to make money, she is also interested in fame, highlighted by the fact that she is constantly trying to get into show business or pen the play, musical, or novel that will instantly catapult her into the stratosphere of the stardom she craves.

I Love Lucy is truly a representation of life in 1950s America, complete with the old values and new ideas that were becoming part of our culture. Women working and earning money; easy and efficient travel; moving away from the place you were born; equality in marriage; and interest in politics, education, and ambition were all changing the American landscape forever. The Ricardos and Mertzes were there at the beginning, and are a perfect snapshot of that era, frozen forever in time as a glimpse of 1950s America.

Flashback to the '50s

1951

President: Harry S. Truman

Vice president: Alben William Barkley

Price of bread: 16¢ per loaf

Price of milk: 92¢ per gallon

Price of eggs: 24¢ per dozen

Price of gasoline: 19¢ per gallon

Price of a car: $1,520

Price of a new home: $9,000

Average annual income: $3,515

Famous births: Lucie Arnaz, Tony Danza (actor), Dan Fogelberg (singer), Tommy Hilfiger (designer), Ed "Too Tall" Jones (NFL player), Dean Paul "Dino" Martin (singer), Sally Ride (astronaut), Kurt Russell (actor), Gordon "Sting" Sumner (singer)

Important world and national events: 22nd Amendment to the U.S. Constitution passed (limiting presidents to two terms); the Atomic Energy Commission built the first nuclear fission reactor power plant; *An American in Paris* wins the Academy Award for Best Picture; the first color television broadcast is made from the Empire State Building; Winston Churchill returns to power in Britain; New York Yankee slugger Joe DiMaggio announces his retirement from baseball.

1952

President: Harry S. Truman

Vice president: Alben William Barkley

Price of bread: 16¢ per loaf

Price of milk: 97¢ per gallon

Price of eggs: 25¢ per dozen

Price of gasoline: 20¢ per gallon

Price of a car: $1,754

Price of a new home: $9,075

Average annual income: $3,850

Famous births: Jimmy Connors (tennis player), Bob Costas (sportscaster), Ben Crenshaw (pro golfer), Dale Earnhardt (race car driver), Liam Neeson (actor), Phoebe Snow (singer), Amy Tan (author), Laurence "Mr. T" Tureaud (actor), Robin Williams (actor)

Important world and national events: U.S. presidential election; Anne Frank's *Diary of a Young Girl* is published in the U.S.; California experiences massive earthquake; the Summer Olympics are held in Helsinki, Finland; U.S. begins bombing North Korean power plants; Puerto Rico becomes a U.S. commonwealth; *The Greatest Show on Earth* wins the Academy Award for Best Picture; Dick Clark hosts the first episode of his famous *American Bandstand*; the Winter Olympics are held in Oslo, Norway; Frosted Flakes and Saran Wrap hit grocery store shelves in markets nationwide.

1953

President: General Dwight David "Ike" Eisenhower

Vice president: Richard Millhouse Nixon

Price of bread: 16¢ per loaf

Price of milk: 94¢ per gallon

Price of eggs: 24¢ per dozen

Price of gasoline: 20¢ per gallon

Price of a car: $1,651

Price of a new home: $9,525

Average annual income: $4,011

Famous births: Desi Arnaz, Jr., Tony Blair (British Prime Minister), Pierce Brosnan (actor), Kathie Lee Gifford (entertainer), Cyndi Lauper (singer), Bobby Rahal (race car driver), Leon Spinks (boxer), Mary Steenburgen (actress), James Taylor (singer)

Important world and national events: Soviet Premier Joseph Stalin dies; Senator John F. Kennedy is married to Jacqueline Bouvier; Edmund Hilary and Tenzing Norgay are the first men to reach the summit of Mount Everest; Ike is sworn in as the thirty-fourth president of the United States; *TV Guide* puts out its first weekly volume; the Korean War ends with a cease-fire agreement; Queen Elizabeth II is crowned in England; *From Here to Eternity* wins the Academy Award for Best Picture; New York City first uses the three-color traffic light.

1954

President: General Dwight David "Ike" Eisenhower

Vice president: Richard Millhouse Nixon

Price of bread: 17¢ per loaf

Price of milk: 92¢ per gallon

Price of eggs: 26¢ per dozen

Price of gasoline: 22¢ per gallon

Price of a car: $1,700

Price of a new home: $10,250

Average annual income: $3,960

Famous births: Chris Evert (tennis pro), Ron Howard (actor/director), Robert Kennedy, Jr. (politician), Freddie Prinze (actor), Patrick Swayze (actor), John Travolta (actor), Denzel Washington (actor), Oprah Winfrey (entrepreneur, TV host)

Important world and national events: The first polio vaccine is given to children in Pittsburgh, Pennsylvania; the construction of Disneyland begins in California; Ed Sullivan and CBS sign a twenty-year contract; British runner Roger Bannister breaks the four-minute mile; *On the Waterfront* wins the Academy Award for Best Picture; the U.S. Supreme Court votes to end segregation in public schools in the *Brown vs. Board of Education* case; *Sports Illustrated* puts out its first issue.

1955

President: General Dwight David "Ike" Eisenhower

Vice president: Richard Millhouse Nixon

Price of bread: 18¢ per loaf

Price of milk: 92¢ per gallon

Price of eggs: 27¢ per dozen

Price of gasoline: 23¢ per gallon

Price of a car: $1,910

Price of a new home: $10,950

Average annual income: $4,137

Famous births: Kevin Costner (actor), Bill Gates (co-founder of Microsoft), Whoopi Goldberg (actress/entertainer), Steve Jobs (co-founder of Apple Computers), Olga Korbut (gymnast), Reba McEntire (singer), Phil Simms (NFL quarterback), Bruce Willis (actor)

Important world and national events: Rosa Parks starts the Montgomery bus boycott when she is arrested for refusing to give up her seat to a white man; "Rock Around the Clock" becomes #1 on the *Billboard* charts; the *Captain Kangaroo* show debuts on television; the U.S. occupation of Japan comes to an end; Israel and Egypt agree to a cease-fire; Winston Churchill retires as British Prime Minister; the first Kentucky Fried Chicken restaurant is launched; *Marty* wins the Academy Award for Best Picture; Disneyland is open for business; the Eastern Block countries sign the Warsaw Pact.

1956

President: General Dwight David "Ike" Eisenhower

Vice president: Richard Millhouse Nixon

Price of bread: 18¢ per loaf

Price of milk: 97¢ per gallon

Price of eggs: 27¢ per dozen

Price of gasoline: 22¢ per gallon

Price of a car: $2,050

Price of a new home: $11,725

Average annual income: $4,454

Famous births: Carrie Fisher (actress), Kenneth "Kenny G" Gorelick (saxophonist), Andy Garcia (actor), Dorothy Hamill (figure skater), Tom Hanks (actor), Joe Montana (NFL quarterback), Martina Navratilova (tennis player), Paula Zahn (news anchor)

Important world and national events: the Summer Olympics are held in Melbourne, Australia; *Around the World in 80 Days* wins the Academy Award for Best Picture; Fidel Castro begins his revolution against the Batista government in Cuba; American actress Grace Kelly marries Prince Rainier of Monaco; the Winter Olympics take place in Cortina, Italy; teenagers John Lennon and Paul McCartney meet for the first time at a church dinner; Martin Luther King, Jr. founds the Southern Christian Leadership Conference; President Eisenhower defeats Adlai Stephenson in the U.S. presidential election; the U.S. Supreme Court outlaws segregation on public transportation.

1957

President: General Dwight David "Ike" Eisenhower

Vice president: Richard Millhouse Nixon

Price of bread: 19¢ per loaf

Price of milk: $1 per gallon

Price of eggs: 28¢ per dozen

Price of gasoline: 24¢ per gallon

Price of a car: $2,157

Price of a new home: $12,225

Average annual income: $4,594

Famous births: Katie Couric (news anchor), Gloria Estefan (singer), Vince Gill (musician), Caroline Grimaldi (Princess of Monaco), Caroline Kennedy (attorney), Matt Lauer (news anchor), Spike Lee (actor), Donny Osmond (entertainer)

Important world and national events: Jackie Robinson retires from baseball; the Soviet Union launches Sputnik, its first satellite, and tests nuclear weapons; the Suez Canal is opened; President Eisenhower suffers a stroke; the U.S. and Canada form the North American Defense Command; Federal troops are sent to Little Rock, Arkansas to protect black students attempting to desegregate Little Rock High School; *The Bridge on the River Kwai* wins the Academy Award for Best Picture; Berry Gordy founds the Motown Record Company; Dr. Seuss publishes his classic story, *The Cat in the Hat*.

Fads and Trends

Davy Crockett coonskin hats	3-D movies
James Dean haircuts	Westerns
Sideburns	Saddle shoes
Rock and roll	Sock hops
Hula hoops	Phone booth stuffing
Frisbees	Black leather jackets
Poodle skirts	Drive-ins
Penny loafers	Roller skates

Popular TV Shows

Arthur Godfrey's Talent Scouts	*The Jack Benny Program*
The Bob Hope Show	*Kukla, Fran, and Ollie*
Captain Kangaroo	*Lassie*
The Danny Thomas Show	*The Life and Legend of Wyatt Earp*
December Bride	*Our Miss Brooks*
Ding Dong School	*Ozzie and Harriet*
The Donna Reed Show	*The Price is Right*
Dragnet	*The $64,000 Question*
The Ed Sullivan Show	*The Red Buttons Show*
Father Knows Best	*The Riflemen*
Gunsmoke	*What's My Line?*
Howdy Doody	*You Bet Your Life*
I've Got a Secret	*Your Hit Parade*
The Honeymooners	*Your Show of Shows*

Popular Musicians

The Ames Brothers	Eddie Fisher
Harry Belafonte	Tennessee Ernie Ford
Tony Bennett	The Four Aces
Chuck Berry	The Four Tops
Pat Boone	Bill Haley and His Comets
Rosemary Clooney	Buddy Holly
Nat King Cole	Dean Martin
Perry Como	Martha and the Vandellas
Bing Crosby	The Miracles
Bobby Darin	Patti Page
Doris Day	The Platters
Fabian	Elvis Presley
Fats Domino	Frank Sinatra

Advertisements show the culture and gender roles of 1950s America:

FOR LUCY RICARDO, ONE OF THE BIGGEST
CELEBRITY WORSHIPPERS OF HER DAY,
THE BROWN DERBY WAS HER MECCA.

Hooray for Hollywood!

In the 1950s, Hollywood was in its heyday. Glamour and romance abounded. Movie stars were young, gorgeous, approachable, and warm toward their fans. Fans read movie magazines, imitated the clothing and hairstyles of their favorites, and went to the theater constantly to see the new releases.

There were so many great movie stars during this era it was hard for anyone to pick a favorite. Female stars included Elizabeth Taylor, Doris Day, Ava Gardner, Audrey Hepburn, Jane Powell, Debbie Reynolds, Katharine Hepburn, Jane Russell, Lana Turner, Grace Kelly, Judy Garland, and Marilyn Monroe. Some of the biggest male stars of the day were Montgomery Clift, Gene Kelly, William Holden, Marlon Brando, John Wayne, Jimmy Stewart, James Dean, Frank Sinatra, Tony Curtis, Danny Kaye, Spencer Tracy, Rock Hudson, Henry Fonda, Kirk Douglas, and Cary Grant.

In 1950, the movie industry was coming out of a period of wartime movies. Hollywood had been very active in many ways during the war, doing its part to make sure democracy prevailed. Many of the biggest stars in Hollywood had enlisted and served, including Jimmy Stewart, Kirk Douglas, Tony Curtis, Gene Autry, Henry Fonda, Mickey Rooney, Jack Lemon, Richard Burton, Clark Gable, Art Carney, Tyrone Power, William Holden, Robert Stack, Burt Lancaster, Robert Montgomery, and Steve McQueen. For the rest who were unable to fight, most, if not all, had helped to raise money by selling war bonds. Patriotic Americans Lucille Ball and Desi Arnaz had traveled to Washington, D.C. and other parts of the country to raise money. Desi had wanted to enlist but an injury and subsequent surgery kept him out of the fight. Instead, Sergeant Arnaz and many other entertainers amused the troops by offering hospitality and putting on shows and musical entertainment to keep their

Harpo Marx

TENNESSEE ERNIE FORD WAS AMONG THE FIRST IN A LONG LINE OF 1950S-ERA CELEBRITIES WHO MADE GUEST APPEARANCES ON *I LOVE LUCY*.

CORNEL WILDE

WILLIAM HOLDEN

ROCK HUDSON

minds off the horrors of war. Desi had also made a couple of war movies, including *The Navy Comes Through* and *Bataan* (receiving an award for the latter).

In the '50s, the country and the world were emerging from the time of war and fear, and entering a time of peace and prosperity. Hollywood was a glamorous place once again. Westerns and musicals were popular, and no longer were movies shot with black and white film. The Hays Code, which had put many restrictions on Hollywood's freedoms, including restrictions on suggestive dancing, interracial marriage, offensive language, and crime, was losing its grip. Studios had gone to court to plead for the right to defy the Code based on First Amendment rights. Movies were getting bolder, sexier, and more controversial. No longer did the good guys always win, and no longer were the police always trustworthy. Fashion was once again beautiful, and movie stars no longer felt they could not dress beautifully because so many were suffering.

There were so many places to go in Hollywood, and tourism was booming. Both locals and out-of-towners visited Hollywood Boulevard, the Sunset Strip, Melrose Boulevard, Rodeo Drive, the Hollywood sign, and the Walk of Fame. Grauman's Chinese Theatre was also a popular place for celebrities and tourists alike. The theater was a place for parties, Academy Award ceremonies, and premieres. Outside the theater, then and now, is the famous walkway where movie stars such as John Wayne, Mary Pickford, Shirley Temple, the Marx Brothers, Jimmy Stewart, Van Johnson, Fred Astaire, and Bob Hope memorialized their hands, feet, and signatures in cement. Thousands of tourists flock there annually to match their prints with those of the stars, just like Lucy and Ethel did on *I Love Lucy*.

Another Hollywood hotspot of the day was the Brown Derby, which was actually a chain of restaurants in Los Angeles so named because the original on Wilshire Boulevard is shaped like a derby hat, and painted brown. The second restaurant, on North Vine Street in Hollywood, is probably the one visited by Lucy and the gang. It is said that Clark Gable proposed to Carole Lombard in the restaurant, and also that the very first Cobb Salad (named after co-owner Robert Cobb) was made there. Besides the attention-grabbing design of the buildings themselves, another interesting feature of the Brown Derby restaurants is the array of caricature drawings of movie stars and other famous celebrities that line the walls. Most of them were drawn by Jack Lane between 1947 and 1985. In the *I Love Lucy* episode in which they go to the Brown Derby, Lucy and her pals enjoy looking at the cartoon drawings of their favorite stars, until Ethel embarrasses herself by asking Eve Arden if the caricature of herself is that

VAN
JOHNSON

of Shelley Winters or Judy Holliday.

Another popular pastime for tourists was to take bus tours of Hollywood star homes. Tanner Grey Line Motor Tours was a famous company that gave such tours. The buses left from the corner of Hollywood and Vine, went past the Brown Derby and Ciro's Restaurant, and into Beverly Hills, where they went past the Beverly Hills Hotel and the homes of stars such as Charles Boyer, Gary Cooper, Rudolph Valentino, Deborah Kerr, Shirley Temple, and Robert Taylor. On the way back, they rode by Schwab's Drug Store and Grauman's Chinese. Lucy and Ethel took a similar tour in the final episode of Season Four. They ended

NANCY KULP

up at the home of Richard Widmark, where Lucy scaled a wall to get a grapefruit, fell off the wall and was unable to get back over. During the taping of this episode, the Arnaz home on Roxbury Drive was filmed as the place where Lucy ran across the yard and climbed up the wall.

Hollywood in the 1950s was full of fans, much like it is today. There were fan magazines containing interviews with the stars, photos of them at home with their families, and opportunities to join fan clubs and receive autographs and signed photos. Young fans of the day were called bobby-soxers, because they wore "bobby," or cuffed ankle socks. This trend began in the 1940s with enthusiastic fans of singer Frank Sinatra. It continued through the next decade, and in the episode "Don Juan is Shelved," Lucy, the Mertzes, and Mother McGilliduddy dress as elderly bobby-soxers to try to persuade MGM that Ricky is wildly popular with his fans.

One distasteful aspect of Hollywood during this era was the HUAC (House Un-American Activities Committee) hearings, which took place in Washington D.C. under the control of the House of Representatives between 1938 and 1975. The committee began as an investigation into people connected with the Nazi or Ku Klux Klan movements. In 1947, it began investigating people in Hollywood who were suspected of having ties to communism. Since the end of World War II and the dividing up of Europe between the

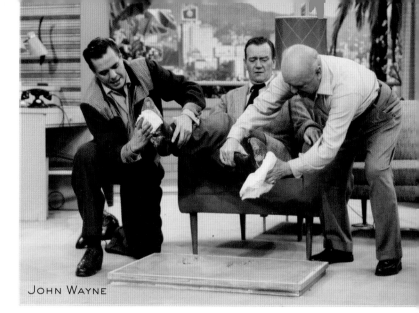

John Wayne

west and the Soviet Union, communism was the new threat to democracy, replacing German fascism. The committee asked the accused the famous question, "Are you now, or have you ever been a member of the communist party?" Most of the original defendants were screenwriters, but celebrities such as composer Aaron Copeland, singer Lena Horne, and actress Judy Holliday were also included. The committee was at its height between 1952 and 1956, when Lucille Ball was called to testify. Back in the early 1930s a young Lucy, along with the rest of her family, had registered as a communist to please her elderly grandfather, Fred Hunt. She never voted for a communist candidate, and the registration expired when she moved away from New York.

George Reeves

Elsa Lancaster

RICHARD CRENNA

Orson Welles

Twenty years later, at the height of her fame and after having recently given birth to her second child, her world almost collapsed under the strain of HUAC. She had been called to testify about her involvement with the communist party, and had been exonerated. Although she had been promised that her testimony and even the fact that she had been called before the committee would remain confidential, someone leaked the story to the press. In early September 1953, Lucy and Desi were forced to explain her past to the press. Their very real fear was that their show would be canceled and that fans would desert them. They would have been social outcasts unable to find work. They might have lost their homes and had their children taken away. Luckily, none of that happened. They explained the situation to some of their pals in the press who printed the story. They were so beloved by their fans and by the public that their show continued to be ranked first in the Nielsen ratings. It was forgotten almost as soon as it happened. As Desi told the studio audience the first time they taped after the story broke, Lucy's hair "is the only thing red about her." Lucy and Desi were lucky; many others in their business suffered life-long blacklisting from their community and from their country.

There were many wonderful things about Hollywood in the decade of the 1950s. Films were being produced, actors had returned from war, censorship was loosening up, and glamour had returned. However, there was also the ugliness

BOB HOPE

CHARLES BOYER

of the HUAC hearings, which put a damper on a fearful population and caused distrust and anger in Hollywood. Happily, the good outweighed the bad, and this decade is remembered as being part of the Golden Age of Hollywood.

RICHARD WIDMARK

DESI AND LUCILLE WERE MARRIED ON NOVEMBER 30, 1940. THIS PHOTO OF THEM WAS TAKEN IN 1941 AT THEIR FIRST HOME, THEIR RANCH IN CHATSWORTH.

Before the Beginning

I Love Lucy has its roots in love and marriage. It's a show based upon family and friendship, and it stars an actual married couple, but that isn't the extent of its association with marriage.

I Love Lucy essentially began as a book, written by Isabel Scott Rorick. Published in 1940, the domestic comedy was entitled *Mr. and Mrs. Cugat: The Record of a Happy Marriage*. In 1942, the book was made into a Paramount film called *Are Husbands Necessary?*, starring Betty Field and Ray Milland. In 1948, CBS Radio developed the book as a radio program with Jell-O as its sponsor. They named their new show *My Favorite Husband*, and Lucille Ball and Richard were hired to be its stars. Lucy played housewife Elizabeth (Liz) and Richard Denning played her banker husband, George Cugat (later Cooper). Bea Benaderet and Gale Gordon played Lucy's gal pal Iris Atterbury and her husband, Rudolph, George's boss. The show took place at 321 Bundy Drive in the fictional town of Sheridan Falls (state not mentioned). The Cugats were promoted as "two people who live together and like it."

The show was originally conceived by a team of writers, Bill Davenport and Frank Fox, and the Cugats were written as a wealthy, socially prominent, and upwardly mobile couple. After the trio of Jess Oppenheimer, Madelyn Pugh, and Bob Carroll, Jr. was hired to be the writing team, they changed the name of the couple to Cooper (so as not to confuse them with bandleader Xavier Cugat). They also made the couple middle class, believing that most of their listening audience would better identify with a wife who didn't have a new dress for every day of the week.

Bob and Madelyn had worked at CBS for a number of years, and became a lifelong writing team during the writing of the radio series. Oppenheimer was the show's producer and head writer. He had been a professional radio comedy writer since the early 1930s, and was responsible for taking the Liz Cugat character and turning her into the Lucy Ricardo character that appeared on television. He made her less urbane and more impulsive and childlike. His Liz Cugat lied and schemed, got into trouble, and made her husband angry. The immediate outcome of the change in names, writing, and characterization was that the show was suddenly a huge hit.

LUCY LOOKS OVER A SCRIPT WITH *MY FAVORITE HUSBAND* WRITER MADELYN PUGH.

After the show was on the air for several months, the CBS brass began to talk about taking the show to television. TV was quickly emerging as a force in national media and they wanted Lucille Ball and Richard Denning to simply move to the exciting new mode of entertainment. CBS Vice President of Programming, Larry Ackerman, and Lucy's agent, Don Sharpe, thought Lucy would be perfect for TV. The radio audiences who watched her record in the studio loved her physical

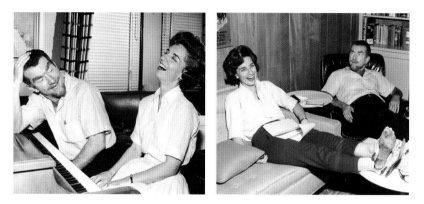

WRITERS MADELYN PUGH AND BOB CARROLL, JR.

comedy and her facial expressions, such as when she made the "eeeewwwww" sound (known to the writers as the "spider" sound). It would be even better if she could use her entire body in slapstick routines, and use props as part of the comedy.

Lucy was interested in making the switch to TV, but wanted her husband to take over the Richard Denning role. Desi had been on the road with his band since the end of

the war. At the end of the 1940s she had finally persuaded Bob Hope to let Desi and his orchestra be Hope's permanent musicians on his popular NBC radio program *The Bob Hope Show*. The couple desperately wanted to start a family, but years of not spending time together in the same zip code had only led to heartbreak, exacerbated by the fact that they endured numerous miscarriages. Lucy was approaching her fortieth birthday and knew there weren't too many years left if she was to make her dream of motherhood come true. She told the CBS honchos that she would do the show only if Desi could play the part of her husband. For many reasons, CBS balked at the idea: Desi was of foreign extraction, had an accent, and was not the all-American Caucasian that Lucy was. He also didn't have the acting background necessary to convince the powers at CBS that he would be able to hold his own with the powerful acting personality that Lucy possessed. They just didn't think it would work.

THE PILOT EPISODE

Lucy, however, thought otherwise, and so did Jess Oppenheimer. She decided to prove her instincts were right by developing a show and taking it across the country to see if the average American audience would buy Lucille Ball and Desi Arnaz as the happily married couple they were. With the help of Desi's friend Pepito Perez, the Spanish clown, as well as Buster Keaton and Lucy's writers, the couple produced a scripted vaudeville-like show complete with musical numbers, dancing, and slapstick comedy, and together they hit the road. They dubbed themselves Desi Arnaz and Band with Lucille Ball, but it was very clear that she was the star of the show. They opened at the Chicago Paramount Theatre on June 2, 1950, with a twenty-minute act, and the press was positive from the get-go: "One of the best bills to play house in recent months. Most of it revolves around Desi Arnaz and his frau, Lucille Ball, who have developed into a sock new act," observed *Variety*.

From there they went to New York City, where they settled in at the Roxy Theatre. It was there that Lucy began to feel ill and very tired. Afraid she was working too hard, Desi sent her to a doctor, who pronounced she was pregnant. From New York, the couple went on to ace reviews in Buffalo and Milwaukee. Unfortunately, due to the physical comedy of the act (at times sliding across the floor on her stomach like a seal), the couple suffered yet another devastating miscarriage. They were more determined than ever to work together and get pregnant again.

Lucy went back to work in films, all the time begging her agent to please find a way for she and Desi to work together. CBS still didn't want any part of a show with Desi, so the couple hired writers to write a different show, about themselves—movie star and an orchestra leader, but once again they thought it would be better to be an average American couple—not wealthy, not famous, not glamorous.

While their professional life remained unsettled in the fall of 1950, Lucy discovered that, at the age of thirty-nine, she was pregnant once again. She decided that the baby was the only important thing and she must to stay home and make sure the child was born healthy. This meant canceling all her contracts, including a coveted role in the upcoming Cecil B. DeMille epic movie *The Greatest Show on Earth*. She also decided that if she couldn't act with Desi, she would never act again. Her life was consumed with being pregnant, taking care of herself, and keeping her husband at home with her. Acting was the last thing on her mind.

Meanwhile, Lucy's agent, Don Sharpe, and Jess Oppenheimer worked on a way to get her back into acting. In the closing days of 1950, as Lucy was home happily gestating, Don was negotiating a deal with CBS for a pilot episode of the newly titled sitcom *I Love Lucy*. They took the premise of *My Favorite Husband*, but turned the Richard Denning banker role into one more apropos for Desi—a nightclub entertainer and bandleader. Lucy would play the role she played on *Husband*—a loving but misbehaving wife—but now there would be an additional aspect to her personality: She wanted to be a star like her husband. Lucy insisted that Jess take the reins as producer, and CBS was happy to let him do so, especially considering his successful career in radio.

CBS was interested in the domestic comedy angle, with the wife trying to break out a bit and the husband trying to keep her at home. During the war, women had gone to work out of necessity, so it was no longer considered unusual or "quaint" for a woman to want a little more than to stay home. Be that as it may, Lucille Ball was very interested in the domestic approach Jess had developed. She loved the old-fashioned storyline of a housewife taking care of her husband, while getting into predicaments and mischief on the side.

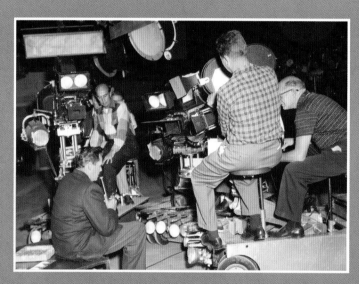

DESI AND CREW USHERED IN MANY NEW TECHNIQUES THAT ARE STILL USED IN TELEVISION PRODUCTION.

DESI "WARMED UP" THE AUDIENCE BEFORE FILMING OF EACH EPISODE.

DIRECTOR MARC DANIELS AND CAMERAMAN KARL FREUND

Oppenheimer and his two radio writers, Pugh and Carroll, used aspects of the radio show as well as Lucy and Desi's vaudeville show to make the audition piece. In this "pilot episode," Ricky had a show to put on and Lucy made herself a part of it by performing the "Professor" role that had delighted crowds when Lucy and Desi went on tour the preceding summer. The first half-hour program was set to debut over closed-circuit TV on March 2, 1951. It would also be kinescoped (the mode of the day of recording programs for television by filming the picture off of a video monitor) for potential sponsors to see later. The kinescope images were blurry, but it was the only effective way of capturing images from live TV at the time.

The pilot was made at CBS headquarters, Studio A, Columbia Square on Sunset and Gower. It had only two sets (a nightclub and the apartment). There were only two actors

beside Lucy and Desi—Jerry Hausner, who would later play Ricky's agent Jerry on *I Love Lucy*, and Desi's pal Pepito the Clown, who had developed the Arnazes' vaudeville act. One large problem that confronted the writers in that first episode was the expanding waistline of their five-months-pregnant star Lucille Ball. Due to her condition, Lucy was kept in bathrobes and oversized tuxedos during the filming. She did her Professor routine that Pepito had devised for her, but without the sliding across the floor seal aspect, now made impossible by her pregnancy.

After filming ended, Lucy and Desi went home and waited. Don Sharpe packed up the film and took it to New York to show to advertisers. He was initially turned down by several of the big ad giants, including Young & Rubicam, before he was finally able to make a deal with the Biow Agency. On April 23, almost two months after

The set of "Ricky Loses His Voice," episode 44.

Behind the scenes with Desi and producer Jess Oppenheimer

LUCILLE AND DESIGNER
ELOIS JENSSEN

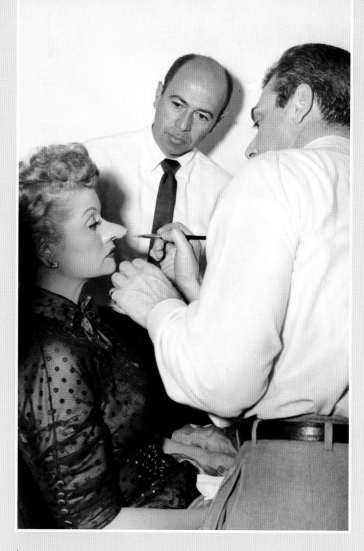

filming the pilot, the show was picked up by one of Biow's clients, Philip Morris Cigarettes. The weekly show would air on Monday nights starting in October. Due to the proposed schedule, it was clear that Lucille would be forced to give up her film career in favor of this new television occupation. She knew what was at stake. If she didn't do it, she might lose her marriage, and she was weeks away from giving birth. If she did do it, she might fail and then it would be very difficult to get back into motion pictures. It was a gamble Lucy was willing to take.

Problems arose immediately, the first when Jess received a call from the Biow Agency inquiring when everyone involved in the show would be moving to New York. The Arnazes were not willing to leave their home, especially considering the impending birth of their first baby. Jess expressed his dismay; this was not part of the bargain. The agency, on the other hand, did not wish to have its New York audience have only kinescoped versions of the show. They wanted the shows to be filmed in Hollywood, or be produced live in New York. Lucy and Desi stood their ground, insisting they film in Los Angeles or there would be no show. They reached a tentative agreement wherein the first few shows would be filmed in Hollywood, but if the kinescope versions were sub par, they would have to move production to New York. Of course,

putting the shows on film would be much more costly than making them live. Desi solved the problem by agreeing that he and Lucy take a salary cut of $1,000 per episode, but as part of the bargain they would own 100 percent of the series. CBS and Philip Morris readily agreed to the deal.

The next hurdle the couple needed to overcome was figuring out where they would film the show. Knowing that his wife worked best in front of a live audience, Desi was determined to provide one for her. The team of writers and directors considered rehearsing in front of a live audience and using their laugh tracks but decided against it. Working against the clock and against the grain, Desi turned to Al Simon and Hal Hudson who, along with Desi, developed the idea for filming the show with multiple 35mm cameras before a live audience. Before they could do anything though, they had to find a place to film. They searched

all over Los Angeles for an appropriate place, but no one was able to provide them with the space and construction allowances they needed.

Finally, with only a week to spare before rehearsals began, Al Simon met with the owner of General Service Studios, a seven-acre lot at 1040 North Las Palmas Avenue. They agreed on a price of $1,000 per week to rent Studio Two (thereafter called the Desilu Playhouse) for the filming of fifty-two episodes, and Desi added his blessing to the deal a few days later when he toured the venue. CBS fronted Desilu Productions $25,000 to renovate the studio, including set design, plumbing, electrical, carpentry, lighting features, and adding bleachers for the audience.

Desi had hired Oscar-winning lighting designer Karl Freund for the show. Rather than setting up lights on poles, that lit parts of the stage at a time, Freund designed an

overhead lighting assemblage that lit the entire stage evenly. The wooden floor was torn up and replaced with one that would allow the multiple camera dollies to move swiftly and silently over the surface. Everything finally appeared to be in place from a technical standpoint.

All the while, a frantic search for personnel was taking place. The writers had decided that the Ricardos needed a couple to play "second banana," like the Atterburys had done for the Coopers of *My Favorite Husband*. They decided on another married couple, older, so they could be parental figures for the younger Ricardos, but not too old that they couldn't also be pals. They named them Ethel and Fred Mertz. Much to Lucy's dismay, *My Favorite Husband* alum Gale Gordon was busy with his show *Our Miss Brooks*, so he could not be cast.

Then an old vaudevillian and veteran of over a hundred

movies, actor William Frawley, entered the running. Frawley was having a tough time getting hired in Hollywood because of his reputation for being a heavy drinker, and being late or missing filming all together. While Lucy was at home preparing for the impending birth of her daughter, she received a phone call from the sixty-year-old actor, asking about a role in her new TV show. She and Frawley had appeared in the same film, *Ziegfeld Follies* (1946), but did not know each other well. Lucy and Desi thought he would be a great asset to the show, given his considerable experience with movie making, but CBS and Philip Morris balked at the idea. Desi didn't take no for an answer, however, and struck a deal with his choice to play best bud Fred. If Frawley were absent or unable to perform even once for anything other than a legitimate health reason, he would be fired. Considering how hard times were for him, Bill immediately agreed to the terms, and Fred Mertz was born.

Ethel was a little harder to find. Since Bill Frawley was sixty years old, his wife had to look as if she was his contemporary. She had to be at least ten years older than Lucy, or look it. She had to be a little frumpy, thus allowing Lucy to take on a more glamorous role alongside her. At the same time, she couldn't be so grandmotherly that she wouldn't be able to join Lucy in her plots and schemes. Many actresses tried out for the role, but none was right. After many discussions with Desi and Jess, director Marc Daniels suddenly thought of a friend of his from his days in New York. Vivian Vance, who, as luck would have it, was performing nearby in the play *The Voice of the Turtle*, would be the perfect foil for the antics of Lucy Ricardo.

Although technically only two years older than Lucy, Vivian could make herself appear older, and she could certainly cut down on the glam when needed. Neither Desi nor Jess had heard of the actress, so along with Marc they

attended a performance of her play on July 28. Lucy was unable to join as she had given birth via caesarean section less than two weeks prior. The three men agreed that Vivian was the perfect Ethel after watching only the first act, leaving Marc to go backstage during intermission and give her the exciting news. Vivian was less than thrilled at the prospect of television. She was a theater actress and had acted in only a couple of films in her life. Marc persuaded her to audition, which she did a week later despite her misgivings. She was hired over the phone just a few weeks before rehearsals began.

Looking back, it seems almost impossible that within a matter of six months, Lucy and Desi shot a pilot; sold a show; developed an entirely new form of capturing that show on film before a live audience; put together a team of writers, producers, directors, designers, cameramen, and crew; found and renovated a studio; found and hired their co-stars; and most importantly to them, gave birth to their first baby, daughter Lucie Desiree Arnaz. With all their ducks finally in a row, the couple took their final leap of faith and burst upon the unsuspecting American public with a show that would very shortly be a number-one hit—*I Love Lucy*.

DINNER BACKSTAGE WITH
DESI'S MOTHER, DOLORES
ARNAZ, AND LUCY'S MOTHER,
DEDE BALL

Getting to Know You

Lucille Esmeralda McGillicuddy Ricardo

Born: West Jamestown, New Yok

Occupations: Housewife, mother, busybody, wanna-be star

Hair: Red (well, sort of)

Eyes: Blue

Enjoys: World travel, matinées, movies, spending money, buying hats, singing, dancing, matchmaking, baking bread, gossiping

Club Affiliations: The Wednesday Afternoon Fine Arts League (co-president)

Nicknames: Miss Never-Say-Die

Talents: Getting into trouble, blabbing secrets, boxing chocolates, stomping grapes, wallpapering, dish washing, arguing with Ricky, getting in on the act, ballet, playing the sax

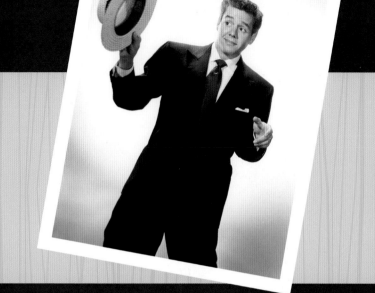

Ricardo Alberto Fernando Ricardo y de Acha

Born: Havana de Cuba

Alternate Name: Enrique Alberto Fernando Ricardo y de Acha

Occupations: Club owner, husband, father, actor, singer, musician, chicken farmer

Hair: Black

Eyes: Brown

Education: Havana University

Enjoys: Telling fairy tales in Spanish, singing, conga playing, boxing matches, fishing, duck hunting, golf

Nicknames: Loverboy, Señor Tightwad, Cuban Skinflint, Peso Pincher

Talents: Saying no, putting together a show, singing, building barbecues, dancing cheek to cheek, designing Parisian fashions, cooking rice

Ethel Louise Roberta Mae Potter Mertz

Born: Albuquerque, New Mexico

Occupations: Vaudevillian, godmother, housewife, actress, landlord

Hair: Blond

Eyes: Blue

Enjoys: Eating, movies, shopping, singing, club meetings, gossiping, world travel

Club Affiliations: Middle East 68th Street Woman's Club, The Wednesday Afternoon Fine Arts League (co-president)

Nicknames: Old Battleaxe, Miss Walkie-Talkie, Big Chief Hog-It-All

Talents: Scheming with Lucy, wallpapering, gossiping, playing bridge, arguing with Fred, selling salad dressing, diner cooking, playing the piano, stealing footprints, party planning, curtsying, being an all-around best gal pal

Frederick Hobart Mertz

Born: Steubenville, Ohio

Occupations: Vaudevillian, godfather, husband, actor, WWI soldier, landlord, chicken farmer

Hair: Gray (what there is of it)

Eyes: Blue

Enjoys: Making and hoarding money, managing buildings and bands, drinking beer, the fights, baseball games, keeping the heat down and raising the rent

Club Affiliations: East 68th Street Athletic and Recreation Society

Talents: 1909 Golden Gloves champ, plumbing, baking cakes, fighting with Ethel, getting hired by Ricky, playing the violin

Nicknames: Beautiful fat old goat, Buster, Second-hand Louey, Buzz Saw, Charm Boy, Fritzi Boy

In real life, these four characters were played by four accomplished entertainers from four different backgrounds who came together at a serendipitous time to create a television legend:

Lucille Desirée Ball

Born: August 6, 1911, Jamestown, New York

Parents: Desirée Eveline Hunt and Henry Durrell Ball

Siblings: Frederick Henry Ball

Spouse: Desi Arnaz (1940–1960, divorce), Gary Morton (1961–1989, her death)

Children: Lucie Desirée Arnaz, Desiderio Alberto Arnaz IV

Show business break: Lucy had been a fashion model for Hattie Carnegie and had posed for portraits. One of the portraits was used as a poster to sell Chesterfield Cigarettes. Agent Sylvia Hahlo was looking for a model to be in the chorus of the movie *Roman Scandals*, and Lucy fit the bill. She was sent from New York to Hollywood for six weeks, and never returned.

Movies: Her more than eighty films include: *Stage Door*; *Room Service*; *Dance, Girl, Dance, Dance*; *Valley of the Sun*; *The Big Street*; *DuBarry Was a Lady*; *Lured*; *Sorrowful Jones*; *The Facts of Life*; *Yours, Mine and Ours*; *Mame*

Television: *I Love Lucy*, *The Lucy Show*, *Here's Lucy*, *Life with Lucy*, many guest appearances

Death: April 26, 1989, acute rupture of abdominal aorta, ashes interred at the Lakeview Cemetery, Jamestown, New York

Hollywood Walk of Fame: 6100 Hollywood Boulevard and 6436 Hollywood Boulevard

Desiderio Alberto Arnaz III

Born: March 2, 1917, Santiago de Cuba

Parents: Dolores (Lolita) Acha and Desiderio Alberto Arnaz II

Siblings: none

Spouse: Lucille Ball (1940–1960, divorce), Edith Mack Hirsch (1963–1985, her death)

Children: Lucie Desirée Arnaz, Desiderio Alberto Arnaz IV

Show business break: Desi formed the Siboney Septet in Miami and was discovered by Xavier Cugat. Cugat sent him to New York to be part of his band, but Desi soon decided to form his own band. He introduced Conga music to New York and was soon the hit of the town. He was tapped for a role in the Broadway musical *Too Many Girls*, which led him to Hollywood to make the movie.

Movies: *Too Many Girls* (with Lucy); *Father Takes a Wife*; *Four Jacks and a Jill*; *The Navy Comes Through*; *Battan*; *Cuban Pete*; *Holiday in Havana*; *The Long, Long, Trailer* (with Lucy); *Forever Darling* (with Lucy)

Television: *I Love Lucy*, many guest appearances

Death: December 2, 1986, cancer, ashes scattered at sea

Hollywood Walk of Fame: 6254 Hollywood Boulevard and 6325½ Hollywood Boulevard

Vivian Roberta Jones

Born: July 26, 1909, Cherryvale, Kansas

Parents: Euphemia Mae Ragan and Robert Andrew Jones

Siblings: Venus, Dorothy, Maxine, Robert Jr., and Lou Ann Jones

Spouse: Joseph Danneck, Jr. (1928–1931, divorce), George Koch (1933–1930, divorce), Philip Ober (1941–1959, divorce), John Dodds (1961–1979, her death)

Children: None

Show business break: Left the Albuquerque Little Theatre to go to New York and try her luck on Broadway. After a couple of years of getting good reviews but being only a chorus girl, Vivian's name was finally in lights on the marquee when she landed the role of Stefanie Stevanova in the play *Hooray for What!* with comic star Ed Wynn.

Theater: *Music in the Air; Anything Goes; Red Hot and Blue; Skylark; Let's Face It; My Daughter, Your Son; The Voice of the Turtle* (all on Broadway)

Movies: *The Secret Fury, The Blue Veil, The Great Race*

Television: *I Love Lucy; The Lucy Show; Here's Lucy* (as guest star), many guest appearances

Death: August 17, 1979, cancer, ashes scattered in San Francisco Bay

Hollywood Walk of Fame: 7000 Hollywood Boulevard

William Clement Frawley

Born: February 27, 1887, Burlington, Iowa

Parents: Mary Ellen Brady and M. A. ("Mike") Frawley

Siblings: John, Paul, and Mary Frawley

Spouse: Edna Louise Broedt (1914–1927, divorce)

Children: None

Show business break: Started his career with his brothers in vaudeville, then in 1915 he played the famed Palace Theatre in New York and at the same time made his film debut in *Lord Loveland Discovers America*. He eventually settled in New York and spent many years in Broadway productions.

Theater: *The Gingham Girl; Merry, Merry; Bye Bye Bonnie; Talk About Girls; She's My Baby; Here's Howe!; Sons O Guns; She Lived Next to the Firehouse; Tell Her the Truth; Twentieth Century; The Ghost Writer* (all Broadway)

Movies: His more than one hundred films include *The Lemon Drop Kid; Three Married Men; Something to Sing About; Huckleberry Finn; The Farmer's Daughter; Ziegfeld Follies; Miracle on 34th Street*

Television: *I Love Lucy; My Three Sons*, many guest appearances

Death: March 3, 1966, heart attack, buried at San Fernando Mission Cemetery, Mission Hills, California

Hollywood Walk of Fame: 6322 Hollywood Boulevard

The Episodes

The *I Love Lucy* show is a domestic comedy based on the comedic talents of Lucille Ball and her co-stars, in plots that depict average characters doing astonishing things and getting themselves into side-splitting situations. The *I Love Lucy* writers created some amazing and memorable plots for the fearsome foursome. How many ordinary New York housewives end up stomping grapes in Italy, rubbing elbows with movie stars, climbing the Empire State Building, or getting drunk on national TV? Not many.

However, most of the *I Love Lucy* plots fall into a few distinct categories, such as Lucy wanting to get into the act or creating a total fiasco. Many of the episodes could actually fall into more than one category, such as needing money and making a mess of things ("The Million-Dollar Idea" or "Lucy is Envious"). Here is a list of all the episodes by theme. As you can see, *I Love Lucy* followed a very simple formula—put extraordinary characters in otherwise ordinary situations, and watch what happens.

WANTED: Fame, Fortune, and Stardom!

The Diet

Filmed September 28, 1951, aired October 29, 1951

Lucy is dying to get a job at Ricky's club, so when she learns that one has opened up, she is determined to get in. She auditions, and Ricky says she can have the job, but she needs to lose twelve pounds to fit into the costume. With Ethel's help, Lucy diets and exercises but still can't fit into the dress. In desperation, she sits in a sweatbox to take off the last few pounds. All her hard work and starvation pay off, but she is so weak she collapses right after the show.

Firsts

- First time Lucy wants to be in the show, claiming to be a great singer and dancer
- First time Lucy uses the name "McGillicuddy"
- First time Ricky gets angry in Spanish
- First time Lucy and Ricky perform at the club
- First time Lucy says "ewwwwwwwwww"
- First (and last) time we see or hear about the Mertzes' dog, Butch

The Audition

Filmed October 12, 1951, aired November 19, 1951

The acting bug has bitten Lucy, so when she learns there will be a talent scout at the club, she begs Ricky to let her perform. As if on cue, Ricky says no, but when one of his acts is injured falling off his bicycle, she is asked to take his place. Dressed up as "The Professor," Lucy does a funny act involving a cello and a "saxovibratrombaphonovitch," which she plays while pretending to be a trained seal. Lucy is offered a contract, which she turns down to stay home with her hubby.

Firsts

- First time Ricky sings "Babalu" and plays the conga
- First time we see the Ricardos' bathroom
- First mention of sponsor Philip Morris
- First time Ricky says "dun't"

The Adagio

Filmed November 23, 1951, aired December 31, 1951

Ricky is debuting a new act at the club—a French Apache dance. Lucy wants to be part of the act, so Fred offers to teach her. Unable to learn anything from Fred, Lucy seeks instruction from a Frenchman who instantly falls in love with her, and expects her to run away with him. Despite his persistence Lucy refuses, but when Ricky finds the man hiding in his home, he decides to cure Lucy of the acting bug by challenging Monsieur Raymond to a duel.

First

- First reference to Ethel's eating habits

The Benefit

Filmed November 30, 1951, aired January 7, 1952

Ethel's club—the Middle East 68th Street Women's Club—is putting on a benefit show, and Lucy wants to be part of the fun. Ethel wants Ricky to headline the entertainment, but Lucy says she will only ask him if she can be in the show, too. Ethel has no choice but to agree to the blackmail, and Ricky finally agrees that he will do a vaudeville song

and dance act with Lucy, but he is not amused when she manages to upstage him and steal all his punch lines.

Firsts

- First time Ethel plays the piano
- First card game
- First time Lucy sings off key

The Ballet

Filmed January 11, 1952, aired February 18, 1952

Ricky is planning a new act at his nightclub, and he needs a pair of ballet dancers and a burlesque comic to fill the bill. Lucy claims that she was once a great dancer, although she hasn't been on her toes for years. She goes to a ballet school for a refresher class, and finds out she needs more practice than she thought. She turns her attention to learning the burlesque act, but when the club calls and says they need her right away, she thinks they need a comic rather than a dancer, and her performance is a big flop.

Firsts

- First time Ricky says, "You cannot be in the show."
- First mention of Mertz and Kurtz

Lucy Does a TV Commercial

Filmed March 28, 1952, aired May 5, 1952

Ricky is going to perform on a TV special, and he needs someone to take the role of the spokesperson for a vitamin tonic. Lucy is dying to be seen on TV, so she begs Ricky to give her a try. When he refuses, she tricks the girl he hired, and goes to the TV studio to do the spot. While rehearsing to sell Vitameatavegamin (a vitamin tonic containing 23 percent alcohol), she gets a bit tipsy. By the time she goes on live TV, she is positively smashed. Ricky has to carry her off stage when she interrupts his performance.

First

- First time Lucy appears on TV

The Saxophone

Filmed June 6, 1952, aired September 22, 1952

Ricky and his band are going on tour, and Lucy wants to be included. When she learns that he needs a saxophone player, she goes up to the attic to dust off the one she hasn't played since her days in the high school marching band in Celoron, New York. She can't play a note so she doesn't get the job, but she decides to make Ricky jealous of a phantom lover so he will decide he can't leave her home alone. As usual, her plan backfires when Ricky figures out her scheme.

Ricky Loses His Voice

Filmed August 22, 1952, aired December 1, 1952

Ricky falls ill right before the big reopening of his night-club. He wants desperately to impress his new boss, Mr. Chambers, but the doctor orders him to stay in bed. Lucy is determined not to let her hubby down in front of the boss, so she and Fred and Ethel put together a vaudeville show straight out of the flapper days of the Roaring Twenties! Ricky is mortified when he sees what the threesome has put together, but Mr. Chambers is enchanted with the show!

Ricky Ricardo-ism

"I think I'm getting a streptococky!"

Lucy's Show Biz Swan Song

Filmed October 17, 1952, aired December 22, 1952

Ricky is sure that mother-to-be Lucy has completely lost her desire to be a star of stage and screen, but Lucy is not so sure. Ricky hires Fred and Ethel to be part of his Gay Nineties revue as part of the barbershop quartet, and the acting bug bites Lucy once again. Ricky says she cannot possibly be part of the act in her condition, but she manages to sneak in anyway by slipping into the barber's chair and filling in as the fourth voice, much to the dismay of the other three.

Ricky Ricardo-ism

"Look, I don't want you to think I'm a tight skate . . . a cheap wad?"

The Indian Show

Filmed April 3, 1953, aired May 4, 1953

Even though she is now a mother, Lucy still yearns to see her name up in lights. Ricky is staging a new Native American-themed show at the Tropicana, and Fred and Ethel are hired to be part of it. Lucy is dying to join them, but what can she do with Little Ricky? When she learns that the woman in one of the numbers would like to spend more time with her own baby, Lucy offers to fill in for her, and does the number with a papoose—containing Little Ricky—strapped to her back.

Ricky Ricardo-isms

"Honey, put your face back where it belongs."

"Those Indians you used to have in this country. The stories about them will really make your blood cuddle."

Ricky's *LIFE* Story

Filmed May 15, 1953, aired October 5, 1953

Ricky gets a three-page spread in *LIFE* magazine, and Lucy is jealous. She says there were no photos of her because Ricky won't allow her to become famous. Fred persuades Ricky to turn the tables on her by offering to make her a star, but then rehearsing her so hard that she has no choice but to give up her dream. His scheme is working fine and Lucy is exhausted, until Fred spills the beans about the plan, and Lucy decides to give Ricky a little taste of his own medicine by upstaging him during his big number, and getting some applause for herself.

Ricky Ricardo-ism

"You might got something, there."

Lucy Tells the Truth

Filmed October 8, 1953, aired November 9, 1953

Little lying Lucy makes a bet with Ricky and the Mertzes that she can go twenty-four hours without telling a fib. Ethel tries to trip her up at a club meeting, but Lucy learns that telling the truth can be refreshing sometimes. She runs into trouble when she decides to audition for a TV show, and finds she must lie in order to pad her nonexistent résumé. She manages to get through the audition when she unwittingly agrees to be the assistant in a hair-raising knife-throwing act.

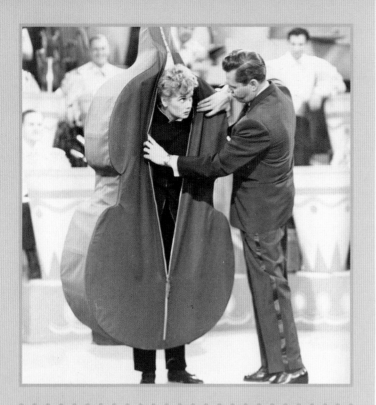

The French Revue

Filmed October 15, 1953, aired November 16, 1953

After eating at a new French restaurant, Ricky is persuaded to put on a French-style act at the Tropicana. Lucy is all excited about the prospect of performing, but Ricky bans her from the club entirely. Determined to be part of the show, Lucy tries to sneak into rehearsal hidden under a lampshade, behind a painting, and even in a bass case. Things don't go her way until she dresses as a dowdy French patron and gets in as an audience member, after which she sheds her costume and appears on stage as a can-can girl.

Ricky Ricardo-ism

"Oh honey, you're 'zagerating."

Lucy Has Her Eyes Examined

Filmed November 12, 1953, aired December 14, 1953

Bill Parker, a pal of Ricky's, is in town auditioning acts for his new Roaring Twenties movie. Lucy, Fred, and Ethel ask for an audition, and Lucy sets out to learn how to jitterbug. She gets lessons from King Kat Walsh, and Parker thinks she and the Mertzes are great, but he wants to see them before an audience. Ricky says they can perform at the club, but on the day of the show Lucy gets sight-altering eye drops from the doctor and as a result her performance doesn't get her the rave reviews she is looking for.

Ricky Ricardo-isms

"People think that I really talk this way, but I dun't."
"Well I suppose that you call it fair to send me out on a wild duck chase for some ice cream that you dun't need."

Home Movies

Filmed January 28, 1954, aired March 1, 1954

Ricky is boring everyone with his home movies of the baby, but when he tells them he is making a pilot film for

a TV show, everyone wants to be included. When Ricky refuses to allow them to take part, Lucy, Ethel, and Fred edit Ricky's footage with their own western extravaganza, complete with slow and fast motion, and even upside down and reverse footage. Ricky is horrified by what Lucy has done to his film, but the producer loves it and thinks Ricky is a genius!

Ricky Ricardo-isms

"Fred, get rid of your head, will you?"

"You have fixed the sheets and blankets, now go take a nap."

Lucy Writes a Novel

Filmed March 4, 1954, aired April 5, 1954

Lucy hopes to become rich and famous by writing the great American novel. She sets out to write a novel with herself as the star, but Ricky and the Mertzes are not thrilled with the way they are portrayed. They seek to stop her from sending the manuscript to the publisher, but she outfoxes them. Her story is rejected by the publisher, causing Lucy to give up the idea of being a writer until another publisher wants to use parts of her story in his book for new authors—in a chapter titled "Don't Let This Happen to You."

Ricky's Movie Offer

Filmed September 16, 1954, aired November 8, 1954

A Hollywood talent scout named Ben Benjamin shows up at the Ricardos'. Thinking he's an intruder, Ethel smacks him over the head with a vase. Lucy arrives home and gets a call that the talent scout is coming over to meet with Ricky, so they fix him up and wait for him to come to. Meanwhile, the news about Ricky's screen test leaks out and the entire neighborhood, including the Mertzes, Mrs. Trumble, and of course Lucy, comes out hoping to be discovered.

Ricky's Screen Test

Filmed September 23, 1954, aired November 15, 1954

Lucy is jumping the gun, deciding where they will live in Hollywood before Ricky even has a screen test. Lucy lobbies to be in the screen test too, hoping she will be discovered as the next big star. Ricky's only concern is that Lucy feed him his lines. On the day of the test, Lucy does her level best to get her face on camera. She frustrates the director to no end, and it looks like Ricky might not even get a decent test until he ties her to her chair so she can't turn around.

Ethel's Home Town

Filmed November 25, 1954, aired January 31, 1955

Driving through Albuquerque, New Mexico, the gang stops in to visit Ethel's father. It seems that Ethel has told her dad that she is going to be a Hollywood star, and the whole town has turned out to make a fuss over her. All this attention on Ethel does not sit well with Ricky, so when Ethel is asked to put on a show, the other three make a plan to upstage her. While she is singing, they perform comedy routines behind her back, much to the delight of the audience.

First

• First time we meet Ethel's family

Lucy Gets in Pictures

Filmed December 16, 1954, aired February 21, 1955

Ricky, Ethel, and Fred are all going to be in movies, and Lucy feels left out. For once Ricky takes pity on her, and gets her a small role in a picture at MGM. Lucy is thrilled, but her costume is top heavy and she can't handle it. She messes up take after take, and each time the director diminishes her role. Finally, he changes the script so she appears already dead in the scene. Leave it to Lucy to make sure her friends know it's her—by writing her name on the bottom of her shoes!

Ricky Ricardo-ism

"Why did you tol' Lillian Appleby that you were gonna be in a movie?"

The Dancing Star

Filmed March 31, 1955, aired May 2, 1955

Lucy has been telling the girls back home about all her celebrity pals, so when Carolyn Appleby shows up in Hollywood, Lucy has to think fast. She begs Van Johnson, who is appearing at the hotel, to allow her to dance with him

in rehearsal. Van gives in and Lucy is thrilled that Carolyn will tell everyone back home. That evening Van calls Lucy to ask her to dance with him that night because his partner is ill. Nervous at first, Lucy is soon a hit with the audience.

Ricky Ricardo-ism

"There is something here that needs 'splainin'."

Lucy and the Dummy

Filmed September 22, 1955, aired October 17, 1955

Ricky would rather go fishing in peace than appear at a party for Metro big wigs. Lucy decides to go to the party without him, and does a comedic dance with a rubber Ricky head attached to a big dummy body. The execs are so impressed with her acting abilities that they offer her a contract! Ricky tells her he thinks it's great that she will be out in Hollywood working while he and Little Ricky and the Mertzes are in New York. Unable to live without her family, Lucy decides to give up show biz after all.

Ricky Ricardo-isms

"You're the one who's impossible. I happen to be very

possible."

"We'll use physiochology."

Lucy Goes to a Rodeo

Filmed October 27, 1955, aired November 28, 1955

Fred's lodge is putting on a western-themed show, and Lucy and Ethel are going to be in it. They practice their singing and dancing with Fred's pal, Rattlesnake Jones. Ricky suffers a crisis when what he thought was a *radio* show turns out to be a *rodeo* show at Madison Square Garden, and he has no acts. Lucy and the Mertzes offer their act for his show—for a price. He finally agrees to let them do their western bell-ringing act in his show, and they're a big hit.

Lucy Meets the Queen

Filmed December 15, 1955, aired January 30, 1956

It's the American invasion of Jolly Ole England. In London, Lucy finds out that Ricky will be performing for the queen at the Palladium, and she insists on being able to perform her practiced curtsey for Her Majesty. Ricky relents and tells her she can be in his circus act, but all her curtsey practice has given her one major charley horse. Despite her pain, Lucy is a hit with the queen, but since her legs are so cramped she must be carried off by two ushers to meet Elizabeth II.

Lucy Meets Orson Welles

Filmed June 14, 1956, aired October 15, 1956

Ricky plans to keep Lucy from finding out that Orson Welles is performing at the club by sending her off to Florida. Lucy runs into the film star and he tells her he was hoping she would assist him with his act. Lucy thinks the Shakespearean actor intends to do *Romeo and Juliet* with her, so she calls her high school acting teacher to tell her about the show. Miss Hannah shows up to see her old student act with the great Welles, but instead Lucy finds herself in the middle of his magic act.

Gals vs. Guys

The Girls Want to go to a Nightclub

Filmed September 15, 1951, aired October 15, 1951

It's the Mertzes' wedding anniversary, and while Ethel thinks an evening of dinner and dancing is in order, Fred prefers a romantic night at the boxing ring. After a heated debate, the gals inform their husbands that they will be going out, and that they won't be unescorted! Ricky and Fred counterattack by trying to get dates of their own, but leave it to Lucy to make sure they end up with two of the worst dates ever—herself and Ethel all dressed up and acting like country folk.

Pioneer Women

Filmed February 22, 1952, aired March 31, 1952

When the wives complain about how hard housework is, the husbands decide to make a bet with them—go back to the year 1900 and see who had it harder, the men or the women. While Lucy and Ethel have to grind their own coffee, bake their own bread, and churn their own butter, Ricky and Fred have to shave with straight razors in cold water, appear in public in 1900s garb, and travel around town on horseback!

Firsts

- First bet between the gals and the guys
- First time on horseback (Ricky)

Men Are Messy

Filmed October 25, 1951, aired December 3, 1951

Lucy is disgusted by Ricky's slobbish ways, so she splits the apartment in half. Her half is neat and tidy while his is "lived in." Ethel sides with Lucy, but Fred prefers Ricky's messier habits. Meanwhile, Ricky's press agent has lined up a photo spread in a magazine, so Lucy decides to teach her hubby a lesson by making the apartment look like a deserted junkyard for the photographer. Too bad for her, the article appears in *Look* magazine—and she is on the cover!

Ricky Ricardo-isms

"'Splain that if you can."

"Esta mujer esta absolutamente loca." ("This woman is absolutely crazy.")

Firsts

- First time Ricky says "ai yi yi!"
- First time Ricky dances (jitterbug)
- First time Lucy gabs on the phone

Lucy's Schedule

Filmed April 18, 1952, aired May 26, 1952

Lucy makes Ricky late for a dinner with his boss, at which he had hoped to ask to be made manager of the Tropicana nightclub. Furious, Ricky develops a rigid time schedule (including timeslots for naps and making phone calls) for Lucy so she will never be late again. At first the schedule seems to be going well, but when Ethel convinces Lucy that Ricky is treating her like a trained seal, Lucy and her gal pals strike back.

Ricky Ricardo-ism

"I'm having dinner with the new bus."

First

• First time Lucy tells Ricky, "I'll be ready in a minute, dear."

Job Switching

Filmed May 30, 1952, aired September 15, 1952

After arguing over who has the harder job—men or women—the gang decides to make a bet to settle the question. So, while the boys stay home to clean and make *arroz con pollo* and chocolate layer cake, the gals get jobs at Kramer's Kandy Kitchen, where they take jobs dipping, wrapping, and boxing chocolates. After failing at all their attempts (and eating several pounds of candy), the wives return home to find their husbands have flunked their test just as badly.

Firsts

• First time guys try to cook anything
• First time gals look for work outside the home

Ricky and Fred Are TV Fans

Filmed May 22, 1953, aired June 22, 1953

Boxing widows Lucy and Ethel are tired of being ignored while their husbands watch pugilism on the TV set. They decide to go out to grab a bite to eat, but find everyone at the diner glued to the fights on TV as well. Lucy needs some change to call home, and when she takes some change from the till, the girls end up getting arrested and accused of being two known criminals. Meanwhile, the boys sit at home, blissfully watching the fights, unaware of their wives' plight.

Equal Rights

Filmed September 24, 1953, aired October 26, 1953

Lucy and Ethel insist on equal treatment from their husbands, so the boys decide to give it to them. They don't help them on with their coats, pull out their chairs, or let them order first. And when the gals have no money to pay for their meals, they end up with nothing but dishpan hands to show for their equality. Lucy and Ethel win in the end though, because when the guys' plan to scare them goes awry, Ricky and Fred end up in the clink.

Ricky Ricardo-ism

"I am the first one to agree that women should have all the rights they want. As long as they stay in their place."

Changing the Boys' Wardrobe

Filmed November 15, 1953, aired December 7, 1953

Lucy and Ethel are sick of their husbands looking less than spectacular. On the other hand, Ricky and Fred like to feel "comfortable." When the wives secretly sell their husbands' ratty old clothes and replace them with new duds, the hubbies fight back. When Ricky is voted one of the ten best-dressed men, Lucy decides to play a trick on him and go to the club dressed as a hobo. Too bad a press photographer is there to take pictures!

Ricky Ricardo-isms

"Besides, this is my best pair of blue gins."

"Nobody's gonna call me Little Frontarooey!"

Ricky Loses His Temper

Filmed January 21, 1954, aired February 22, 1954

When Lucy's hatboxes fill the closet to the brim, Ricky loses his temper. The two make a bet—will Ricky lose his temper before Lucy buys another hat? After Lucy breaks down and buys a new chapeau, she has to use all her tricks to get Ricky to blow his Cuban top before the hat she ordered arrives on the doorstep. Luckily for Lucy, Ricky's even temper saved him a lot of money, so he feels very forgiving about his ruined clothing and lack of sleep, not to mention Lucy's trickery.

The Black Wig

Filmed March 25, 1954, aired April 19, 1954

After watching an Italian movie, Lucy wants to look like a foreign actress. Ricky refuses to let her cut her hair short, so she borrows an "Italian haircut" wig from her hairdresser to try to fool Ricky. Ricky gets wind of her scheme and flirts with the *signorina*. He tries to set up a date, so Lucy decides to trick him. She and Ethel will show up for the date as an Italian lady and a Native-Japanese-Eskimo hybrid!

Ricky Ricardo-ism

"I'll 'splain."

The Golf Game

Filmed April 15, 1954, aired May 17, 1954

Lucy and Ethel are golf widows now that Ricky and Fred have taken to the links. The gals decide that it's best to join 'em since you can't beat 'em, so they tell their hubbies they are going to take up the sport. In order to make it unpalatable for their wives, Ricky and Fred devise a ridiculously complicated game complete with leapfrog and choosing up sides. When the gals meet up with pro Jimmy Demeret, they turn the tables on their sneaky spouses.

First

• First golf game

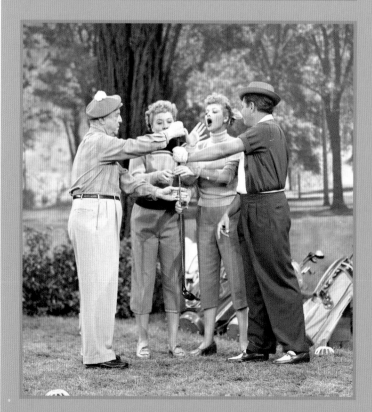

Deep-Sea Fishing

Filmed September 27, 1956, aired November 19, 1956

Lucy and Ethel spend too much money at the Florida shops, so they trick the boys into making a fishing bet. To assure they will win, the gals buy a huge tuna and then try to hide it in the hotel bathroom. Unbeknownst to them, Ricky and Fred have the same idea, and both teams get caught cheating. Onboard the boat the next day, neither team has much luck catching anything until Ricky falls overboard and ends up with fish in his pocket. Lucy reels them both in, winning the day for the girls.

Ricky Ricardo-isms

"I think our boat is a yinx."

"Look Fred, I may speak with an accent, but I don't listen with one."

"What a snicky thin' to do!"

Ricardo vs. Mertz

Breaking the Lease

Filmed January 5, 1952, aired February 11, 1952

When the Ricardos and Mertzes have a silly fight, the Ricardos want to move out, but the Mertzes refuse to let them out of their lease. Finally, Lucy and Ricky make life unbearable when they hold an impromptu concert in their apartment, so Fred and Ethel give in. Once the Ricardos are ready to leave though, everyone breaks down and makes up.

Firsts

- First Ricardo/Mertz fight
- First time Lucy and Ricky want to move out of the building
- First time we see Fred in his PJs (and stocking cap!)
- First time Ricky sings "El Cumbanchero"

The Club Election

Filmed September 12, 1952, aired February 16, 1953

When Ethel is nominated to be president of the women's club, Lucy is jealous so she bribes Carolyn Appleby to nominate her to run against her best friend. What starts out as a friendly campaign soon escalates to some pretty dirty politicking as each lady tries to gather up the necessary number of votes. When it becomes apparent that the entire race depends on one person—the newest member of the club—even the husbands get into the act to try to sway the vote their way.

First

• First club meeting

No Children Allowed

Filmed March 20, 1953, aired April 20, 1953

The baby has been born, and everyone is thrilled but when he keeps up the entire building by crying night after night, Lucy is exhausted and the other tenants are fed up. When a particular neighbor, Mrs. Trumble, complains loudly and often, Lucy is afraid they will have to move. But when Ethel stands up for Lucy, and then retells the story of her heroism ad nauseum to whoever will listen, Lucy gets sick of listening to Saint Ethel, and war breaks out between the BFFs.

Firsts

• First time we meet Mrs. Trumble
• First big Lucy/Ethel fight

The Courtroom

Filmed August 8, 1952, aired November 10, 1952

In honor of their wedding anniversary, Lucy and Ricky present the Mertzes with a new television set. When Ricky breaks it while trying to adjust the wiring, Fred gets furious and puts his foot through the set belonging to the Ricardos! This means war, with each side suing the other. The foursome lands in a courtroom, each trying to convince the judge they are innocent. In the end, they each agree to pay to fix their own TVs, and all is well once again.

Never Do Business with Friends

Filmed May 29, 1953, aired June 29, 1953

Hanging out the laundry to dry in the kitchen starts to wear on Lucy, so she begs Ricky to buy her a clothes dryer. She is thrilled when he buys her not only a dryer but a new washer, too! Ethel asks if she can buy Lucy's old washer, and Lucy says yes, in spite of Ricky's disapproval. When the old washer erupts during its first day of use, the Mertzes refuse to pay for it, but the Ricardos refuse to take it back. However, when someone offers to pay for it, suddenly they both claim ownership.

Ricky Ricardo-ism

"Dryers are too 'spensive."

Firsts

- First mention of Albuquerque (Ethel's hometown)
- First time Ricky says, "Honey I'm home!"
- First time we hear Mrs. Trumble's first name—Matilda

The Diner

Filmed March 18, 1954, aired April 26, 1954

Ricky wants to be his own boss, so the Ricardos and Mertzes go into the restaurant business together. Ethel and Fred, having once worked in a diner, have the "know how," and Ricky has "the name." All goes well until the Mertzes get tired of being treated like the hired help in the kitchen while Lucy and Ricky have all the fun hosting out front—so they

split everything right down the middle. Neither side gets any business, and it looks like a bust until the man who sold it to them agrees to buy it back, for less than they paid for it!

The Sublease

Filmed April 22, 1954, aired May 24, 1954

Ricky has a fabulous two-month summer gig in Maine, and the Ricardos are going to sublet. When Ethel and Fred find out their chums are going to make $350 by renting their place out, they get their noses in a twist and refuse all tenants. They decide to split the profits and rent the place to

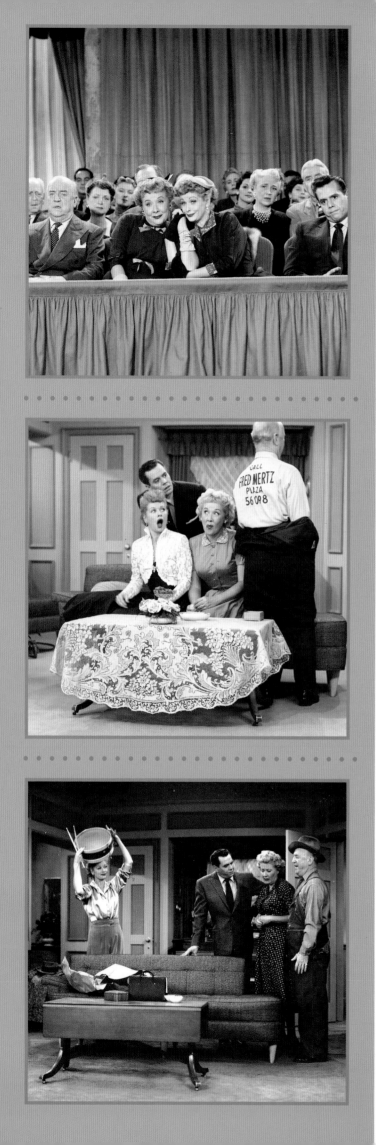

a murder witness. When Ricky's job falls through, they are forced to stay with the Mertzes, and too much togetherness puts a strain on their friendship. Finally, they scare the tenant away, but by then Ricky has gotten another summer job!

Ricky Ricardo-ism

"They're trying to make us look at this thin' through a sweater."

Ethel's Birthday

Filmed October 7, 1954, aired November 29, 1954

It's Ethel's birthday and Ricky is treating everyone to dinner out and a show. Fred asks Lucy to buy a gift for her from him. Even though Lucy knows Ethel wants a toaster, Lucy buys a pair of Harlequin design hostess pants that Ethel thinks look ridiculous. Lucy's feelings are hurt and the two have a fight. They stay mad all week, and refuse to sit together at the theater. When they hear the message of the play—the importance of friends—they kiss and make up.

The Ricardos Are Interviewed

Filmed October 20, 1955, aired November 14, 1955

Ricky's new agent thinks the Ricardos should move into a swanky, expensive apartment befitting a film star. They want to stay where they are, but Lucy goes to check out the posh places anyway. When Ethel and Fred hear of it, they make plans to rent the Ricardos' apartment. Soon they are at each other's throats over the issue of moving out, and when they are all interviewed on national TV, the four of them start arguing, but work out their misunderstandings and make up.

Little Ricky Learns to Play the Drums

Filmed June 28, 1956, aired October 8, 1956

Lucy wants her son to be a doctor but Ricky thinks he possesses musical talent so he buys him a drum. Little Ricky takes to the drums quickly but he seems to have only one slow, monotonous beat. When godparents Fred and Ethel gently suggest that the Ricardos give their son a break from drumming, a fight develops between the friends that causes the boy to run away from home. They find him asleep on the Mertzes' couch wearing earmuffs to shield his ears from the fighting.

First

• First time Little Ricky plays the drums

✳ Marital Woes ✳

Be a Pal

Filmed September 21, 1951, aired October 22, 1951

Afraid her marriage is in trouble, Lucy is desperate to make Ricky fall in love with her all over again. After reading *How to Keep the Honeymoon from Ending*, she first tries her hand at being alluringly feminine at breakfast. When Ricky pays her no attention, she then tries to be his pal by joining in his poker game. She only manages to make him angry by winning the game, so in desperation she attempts to recreate his carefree Cuban childhood, complete with a Carmen Miranda imitation dance, and palm tree in the living room.

Firsts

• First look at the Mertz apartment

• First time the Ricardos' toaster sends bread flying through the air

Fred and Ethel Fight

Filmed January 30, 1952, aired March 10, 1952

The Mertzes are not speaking to each other, and it looks like they might be splitting up, so Lucy jumps into gear and tries to bring them together. Her plan succeeds, but then she and Ricky end up in a huge fight of their own, causing Ricky to move out. Wanting to get him back, Lucy plays the sympathy card, pretending she has been hit by a bus, while Ricky tries to act like a hero by faking a building fire and rushing in to save her.

Ricky Ricardo-ism

"The cast is dead."

Firsts

• First big Ethel/Fred fight

• First mention of henna rinse

• First mention of Lucy's full name (Lucille Esmeralda McGillicuddy Ricardo)

The Marriage License

Filmed February 28, 1952, aired April 7, 1952

When Lucy scrutinizes her marriage certificate, she realizes the clerk made a mistake, writing Ricky's name as "Bicardi." When she is told that the error makes her marriage invalid, Lucy determines to get married again. She makes Ricky take her to the same place and repeat the same proposal, but when things turn sour she changes her mind. Afraid she will leave him for good, Ricky makes a sincere proposal, and they are pronounced husband and wife, again.

Ricky Ricardo-ism

"Well, whatsa matter? Dun't tell me it's expire!"

Firsts

• First picnic

• First time someone says, "Call for Philip Morris!"

Vacation from Marriage

Filmed August 1, 1952, aired October 27, 1952

With their marriages "in a rut," the Ricardos and Mertzes decide a trial separation is in order. Lucy moves in with Ethel, and Fred stays with Ricky. After a day or so, they start to miss their spouses, but no one wants to admit it. Instead, Lucy and Ethel pretend to have a wonderful time dating other men, while the guys take the bait and pretend the same. When Lucy and Ethel are forced to hide on the roof so the guys won't find them at home, they are locked out and left in the cold.

Firsts

• First time anyone is on the roof

• First (and last) time we see the Mertzes' bedroom

The Charm School

Filmed December 10, 1953, aired January 25, 1954

Lucy and Ethel are afraid their marriages are in a rut. After witnessing their husbands pay an extraordinary amount of attention to their single friend's glamorous date, they enroll in a school that promises to turn them into fascinating, unforgettable women. They learn how to walk, dress, do their hair, and apply makeup perfectly, but when they proudly show their husbands what they have become, Ricky and Fred tell them they like them the way they were.

Ricky Ricardo-ism

"Lucy, 'splain!"

The Matchmaker

Filmed June 10, 1954, aired October 25, 1954

Lucy hopes to help her friend Dorothy move closer to a proposal from her boyfriend, Sam. She invites the slow-moving couple over for dinner, hoping to show them a perfect, loving family evening. Instead, Ricky is crabby, the baby is fussy, and her lovely dinner is burned to a crisp. Her meddling causes Ricky to storm off in a huff, but all is eventually well when the Ricardos receive a telegram from Sam and Dorothy saying they are getting married.

Hollywood Anniversary

Filmed February 24, 1955, aired April 4, 1955

Ricky has forgotten the date of his wedding anniversary, and he goes to great lengths to find it out, eventually calling the Greenwich, Connecticut license bureau. Meanwhile, so Lucy doesn't find out he forgot, he pretends that he has planned a huge party for her and invited tons of movie stars. When Lucy finds out the truth she is hurt, and when Ricky goes to the club for their party she refuses to go. She shows up later with Mother, and Ricky sings an apology to her.

Ricky Ricardo-ism

"None of those peoples are coming."

Don Juan and the Starlets

Filmed December 9, 1954, aired February 14, 1955

Ricky has to take publicity photos with his lovely young co-stars, and Lucy is not amused. She is further put out when she does not receive an invitation to accompany him to a movie premiere. Instead, she stays home and falls asleep on the couch, and when Ricky is not in his bed in the morning, she thinks he's been partying all night! Fred lies that Ricky slept on their couch, which makes matters even worse. It takes a maid and a forgotten program to clear the matter up.

Ricky Ricardo-ism

"Did you made that bed?"

In Palm Springs

Filmed March 17, 1955, aired April 25, 1955

The Ricardos and Mertzes are driving each other crazy. Lucy stirs her coffee endlessly, Ricky taps his fingers constantly, Fred is forever playing with his keys, and Ethel eats loudly. Because of their bickering they decide that the gals will go to Palm Springs and the fellas will stay home. After a day or two they start to miss each other, so Ricky asks his pal, Rock Hudson, to tell the wives a story about a couple who fought over little habits. In the end they all realize they've been silly.

Ricky Ricardo-ism

"May I say that you're not the only one that has their tith on etch."

The Fox Hunt

Filmed December 22, 1955, aired February 6, 1956

The green-eyed monster has bitten Lucy again. This time it's a young British actress who has taken a fancy to her hubby. While spending the weekend at the lady's family estate Lucy is constantly left out of the fun. Learning that Ricky is going to go off fox hunting with the girl, Lucy schemes to be right alongside them. The trouble is that Lucy hasn't ever ridden a horse before, and once she manages to get on she rides off backwards, and somehow ends up in a bush.

Country Club Dance

Filmed March 21, 1957, aired April 22, 1957

Lucy, Ethel, and Betty Ramsey are seeing red when their hubbies dance all night with a glamorous young houseguest. Determined to show her up, Lucy puts on a skin-tight dress, Ethel tries a new hairdo, and Betty bathes in perfume. Realizing what they are doing, the boys try their best to pay attention to their wives, but then the gals just think they are up to something. It turns out that the husbands had quickly tired of the young lady, and are happy to go home with their wives.

Ricky Ricardo-isms

"Somebody opened a hole in this paper."
"Well, if you didn't do it, and I didn't do it, who dood it?"

First

• First visit to a country club

Causing Trouble and Crazy Schemes

The Fur Coat

Filmed November 9, 1951, aired December 10, 1951

Ricky has to rent a $3,500 mink coat for an act at the club, but when Lucy finds it she thinks it's her anniversary present. She is so thrilled that she refuses to take the coat off, even when she does housework and goes to sleep! Ricky and Fred cook up a scheme to make her think the coat has been stolen, and when she finds out she has been tricked, Lucy turns the tables on her terrified hubby by pretending to shred the costly coat before his very eyes.

Firsts

- First time Ricky says, "Lucy, I'm home!"
- First time Fred does repair work
- First time Ricky gives Lucy an anniversary gift (even though it wasn't their anniversary)

Lucy Plays Cupid

Filmed December 13, 1951, aired January 21, 1952

Matchmaker Lucy learns her neighbor Miss Lewis has a crush on the grocer. She decides to help her elderly friend land her man by acting as a go-between for the shy spinster. Unfortunately, Mr. Ritter misunderstands and thinks Lucy is the one with an eye for him, so Lucy is forced to invite him over and make herself very unappealing by being a terrible housekeeper and cook, and introducing him to more than two dozen children she claims are hers.

Ricky Ricardo-ism

"I've been 'spectin' this for some time."

Lucy Fakes Illness

Filmed December 18, 1951, aired January 28, 1952

Lucy wants Ricky to feel sorry for her so he'll let her be in the act, so she decides she needs to fake an illness in order to gain his sympathy. At first Ricky is afraid his wife is in trouble, and wants to contact a psychiatrist, but Fred tells him Lucy is faking so he turns the tables on her and convinces her she is dying of the dreaded "gobloots" illness. Lucy is terrified until she catches on that Ricky has played a dirty trick on her, and now it's his turn to feel sick.

Ricky Ricardo-ism

"Could it possibly be that you're suffering from magnesia?"

Firsts

- First use of the furnace pipe to snoop—by Fred!
- First time beds are separated (prior to this, they slept in twin beds pushed together)

The Moustache

Filmed February 8, 1952, aired March 17, 1952

Lucy does not care for Ricky's new moustache, but he intends to keep growing it because he would like to be considered for a role in a movie, and he thinks it makes him look the part. Lucy thinks she can prove to him how ridiculous he looks by gluing a fake beard and moustache to her face, but when the glue won't come off the joke is on her. When the talent scout meets with Ricky, Lucy tries to audition for a role herself, but instead her facial hair horrifies the poor man.

First

• First time Ricky is up for a movie role

Cuban Pals

Filmed March 14, 1952, aired April 21, 1952

When Lucy learns that the lovely Renita, a Cuban dancer Ricky used to dance with, is in town, she is terrified that Ricky will leave her for the beautiful young *señorita*. Lucy goes as far as to sneak into the club dressed as a maid to watch the pair rehearse. In order to make sure they never dance together again, Lucy schemes to have the girl driven out of town (by "cab driver" Fred), and she herself appears as the dancer in Ricky's passionate show.

The Publicity Agent

Filmed April 4, 1952, aired May 12, 1952

Ricky is upset that he isn't getting enough publicity. Other entertainers have fans who will follow them to the four corners of the earth, but he has no one. Determined to make her husband get the exposure he needs, Lucy takes on the role of the Maharincess of Franistan, a royal foreigner who is Ricky's biggest fan. Ricky figures out her plot and turns the tables on her by making her think she is in the middle of a dangerous international incident with deadly consequences.

Ricky Thinks He's Getting Bald

Filmed April 25, 1952, aired June 2, 1952

Afraid he is losing his hair, Ricky is ashamed to take his hat off, even at home. Wanting to prove to him that he still has a thick head of hair, Lucy schemes to throw a party and surround him with bald men, but he doesn't come home until they have all left. Her next plan is to give him painful, ridiculous scalp treatments that she is sure he will never allow her to perform more than once, but the joke is on her when he likes them, and thinks they will work!

Ricky Asks for a Raise

Filmed May 2, 1952, aired June 9, 1952

Ricky wants to ask Mr. Littlefield for a raise, but when the boss refuses him, Ricky quits on the spot. The bandleader thinks his boss won't be able to replace him, but when he does, Lucy springs into action. Making enough reservations to fill every seat in the house, Lucy and the Mertzes then dress up as patrons who, when they hear Ricky is no longer there, walk out in a huff, saying they only came to hear Ricky Ricardo.

Ricky Ricardo-isms

"How does it feel to be married to an also-been?"

"Okay, I quit! K-W-I-T, quit!"

The Handcuffs

Filmed May 16, 1952, aired October 6, 1952

Lucy is tired of her husband having to go out every night to work in a nightclub, so one evening she takes a pair of Fred's trick handcuffs, and cuffs herself to her man. Unfortunately, the cuffs turn out to be the real deal, and she has to find a locksmith to separate herself from Ricky before he has to perform on live television. The locksmith is unable to locate the correct key, so Ricky has to go on TV with one of Lucy's arms acting as his own.

Lucy Changes Her Mind

Filmed September 26, 1952, aired March 30, 1953

Lucy changes her mind about everything—what to wear, what movie to see, what to eat. Ricky is fed up with her indecision and says she never finishes anything she starts, so she makes up her mind to finish everything she has ever begun. She finds an old love letter she never finished and decides to trick Ricky into thinking she never broke things off with a former beau. Wanting Ricky to seethe with envy, she tricks him into watching her flirt—with a dresser's mannequin.

Ricky Ricardo-isms

"Every time you act like this, you must have an interior motive."

"I'm just gonna let her stew in her own goose for a while."

"You know Fred, I think she's really jumped her trolley."

Ricky Has Labor Pains

Filmed October 31, 1952, aired January 5, 1953

Lucy is pregnant so everyone is paying a great deal of attention to her. Her friends are throwing parties for her, and she is receiving gifts while at the same time she is totally forgetting her husband and his needs. Lucy and Ethel decide that Ricky needs some attention, so they ask Fred to throw him a daddy shower, but then Lucy gets worried that the party is going to turn into a wild night of drinking and women, so she disguises herself as a reporter to see for herself.

Lucy Becomes a Sculptress

Filmed November 7, 1952, aired January 12, 1953

Lucy wants her unborn baby to be surrounded by art and culture, but she is afraid the tike will see her as completely untalented in that area. She determines to become a great artist and takes up sculpting, but she is no Michelangelo. When Ricky tells her he will invite an art critic to the house to critique her work, she encases her head in clay so it looks like she has made a perfect likeness of herself. The art critic is enchanted, until he tries to take the "sculpture" home!

Lucy's Club Dance

Filmed March 11, 1954, aired April 12, 1954

The Wednesday Afternoon Fine Arts League has a paltry $1.14 in the bank, so they vote to have a dinner dance fundraiser. They form their own "all-girl orchestra." They are terrible; Ricky tries to help them learn at least one song, to no avail. After Ricky's agent leaks the news of Ricky and his female band, Ricky is forced to go on with the show, but using his own masculine band—in drag—posing as the female musicians.

Lucy Hires a Maid

Filmed March 27, 1953, aired April 27, 1953

Lucy is exhausted from all the extra work she has after the baby arrives. Too tired to do anything fun, she even falls asleep standing upright. Ricky admits she needs help and tells her to hire a maid. The maid that arrives is bossy, and Lucy is intimidated by her forceful personality. It turns out that Lucy is stuck doing as much of the housework as she did before. She schemes to get rid of the maid by making a huge mess, but then finds out that Ricky already let the woman go!

Tennessee Ernie Hangs On

Filmed April 8, 1954, aired May 10, 1954

The Ricardos are desperate to get rid of Cousin Ernie, their bottomless pit of a houseguest. Attempts at giving him a bus ticket home and pretending to be totally broke are complete failures, so they eventually decide there is nothing to be done but let him drive them into the poorhouse. When Ernie gets them all a job performing on *Millikan's Chicken-Mash Hour*, they take it only because with the money they earn, Ernie can catch the bus home—yee haw!

Lucy's Mother-in-Law

Filmed September 30, 1954, aired November 22, 1954

Mama Ricardo is coming from Cuba! She doesn't speak any English, so she and Lucy have trouble communicating until Lucy enlists the help of Professor Bonanova. He hides in the kitchen and tells Lucy what to say in Spanish through hidden microphones. Everyone is very impressed with Lucy's grasp of the language until the professor has to dash off, and Lucy is left speechless. Lucky for her, Mama is touched that she would go to so much trouble to please her.

Firsts

- First time Lucy meets her mother-in-law
- First time Lucy really tries to speak Spanish

Ricky's Contract

Filmed October 14, 1954, aired December 6, 1954

It's been two weeks since his screen test and Ricky is growing more desperate every day. He refuses to leave home unless he has to, or even walk around without his hand on a telephone. One day when Ethel is babysitting, a well-meaning Fred writes out a phone message for Ricky that Hollywood called and he got the job! Ethel can't believe he would do such a dumb thing, but when Lucy sees it, she tells everyone she knows that Ricky's going to be a star. It's a good thing Ricky really did get a call from Hollywood at the club!

Tennessee Bound

Filmed November 18, 1954, aired January 24,1955

While driving through Bent Fork, Tennessee (hometown of the famous Ernie Ford), Ricky gets a speeding ticket. When Lucy sasses the sheriff, he throws her in the clink! Ernie shows up with files, and they saw through the bars while he sings. The sheriff decides to let Lucy out, but when he sees what they've done, he throws them all in jail. It takes a proposal to one of his daughters, a promise to take his twins to Hollywood, and a tricky square dance to get the gang on the road again.

The Hedda Hopper Story

Filmed February 3, 1955, aired March 14, 1955

Mother and Little Ricky have finally arrived from New York. Mother talks about the lovely lady she met on the plane who wants to do a story on Ricky. Meanwhile, Ricky's press agent is trying to get him into Hedda Hopper's gossip column, so he concocts a scheme that has Lucy jumping into the hotel pool, and Ricky rescuing her, all in front of Hedda. The plan is a bust, and when they get back up to their room, who is having tea with Mother? Her pal from the plane, Hedda Hopper!

Ricky Ricardo-isms

"Listen to me, Ethel, the sun opens in the east and it closes in the west."

"Well, you might got somethin' there."

Don Juan is Shelved

Filmed February 10, 1955, aired March 21, 1955

Variety reports that Ricky's film is being canceled and everyone gets into gear to save Ricky's job. Lucy, Ethel, and Mother write five hundred fan letters, and Lucy finds a man she thinks is an actor to play the part of a producer. She wants this man to pretend to be a producer who wants to hire Ricky. Too bad for Lucy she picks the actual Dore Schary, studio chief of MGM, to play himself! Dore tells Ricky they want to put him in another film, and then he leaves without letting Ricky know what Lucy did.

Ricky Ricardo-isms

"Metro just gave me the door in the fence."

"They're shovelin' the picture."

The Star Upstairs

Filmed March 4, 1955, aired April 18, 1955

Lucy is looking to spot her one hundredth movie star in the flesh, so when she finds out Cornel Wilde is in the room above hers she plans to sneak a peek. First she borrows the bellboy's uniform, but Cornel is in the bath. Then she sneaks in under the room service cart, but can't catch a glimpse of the star. When she is locked out on the balcony, she has no choice but to go over the side by tying towels together and jumping. When the film star sees evidence of a prowler in his room, he moves out!

Harpo Marx

Filmed March 24, 1955, aired May 9, 1955

Carolyn Appleby is in town and Lucy's in trouble. It seems she's been fibbing about hobnobbing with movie stars, and she now needs to come up with some to impress her gabby friend. Lucy schemes to steal Carolyn's glasses, and then dresses up as some movie stars in masks and costumes that fool the acutely near-sighted Carolyn. When Ricky asks the real Harpo Marx to go up to his suite and surprise Lucy, Harpo is as surprised as she is when she appears dressed as him!

The Tour

Filmed April 14, 1955, aired May 30, 1955

Lucy and Ethel decide to take a bus tour of movie stars' homes. When the tour drives by Richard Widmark's house, Lucy announces that her husband is having lunch with the star. She and Ethel get off the bus to get a souvenir grapefruit from his tree, but Lucy falls over the wall and has to go into the house. She hides out in his living room until he comes home—with Ricky in tow! She is discovered by the dog, hiding under a bearskin rug, and has to do some fast talking.

Ricky Ricardo-ism

"I am not, positively, absolutely, taking you with me—definitely."

Lucy Visits Grauman's

Filmed September 9, 1955, aired October 3, 1955

While at the famous Grauman's Chinese Theatre, Lucy notices that the cement block containing John Wayne's footprints and signature is loose. What's a girl to do but steal it and try to take it back to New York! Enlisting Ethel's help in the heist, Lucy trips and ends up with her foot in a bucket of hardening cement. Somehow they manage to get the cement piece back to the hotel, but when Ricky finds out what they did, he hits the ceiling. And when the cement shatters—uh oh.

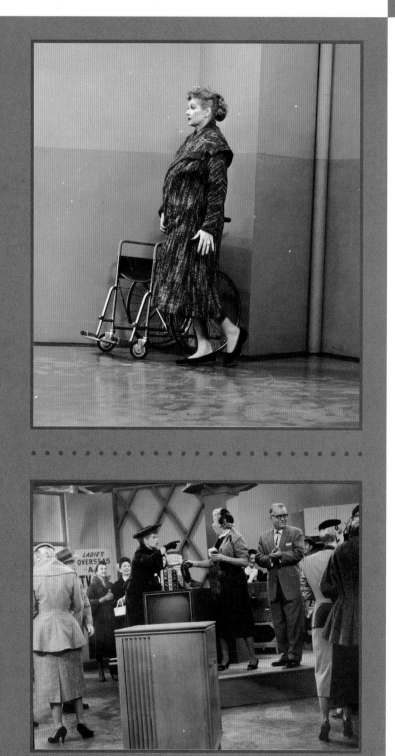

Nursery School

Filmed November 3, 1955, aired December 5, 1955

As much as it upsets Lucy, it's time for Little Ricky to start going to nursery school. Lucy fights the inevitable, refusing to take him, and then hiding him so Ricky can't find him. Little Ricky loves nursery school but he soon comes down with a case of tonsillitis and the doctor recommends surgery. When Lucy is told she can't spend the night with her baby, she masquerades as a pregnant woman, and later as a nurse run amuck, to try to sneak in and comfort her little boy.

Ricky Ricardo-ism

"I'd never know anything around here if you didn't come up once in a while and spin the beans out of the cat bag."

Ricky's European Booking

Filmed November 10, 1955, aired December 12, 1955

Ricky has a contract for he and his band to go on a three-week tour of Europe, and Lucy thinks she is going. When Ricky tells her the truth—that he can't afford to take her along—she devises a scheme to get both herself and Ethel across "the pond." They make up a phony charity, the Ladies Overseas Aid, and plan a raffle. When the district attorney tells Lucy that what she's done is illegal, she has to cancel the raffle and turn the money over to a legitimate charity, or go to jail!

Ricky Ricardo-ism

"Wha' happun?"

Bon Voyage

Filmed December 1, 1955, aired January 16, 1956

It's time for the gang to heave ho and weigh anchor on their European adventure. All set and ready to go, Lucy just has to kiss Little Ricky one last time. Her timing could not be worse when she gets her skirt stuck in the chain of a delivery bike just as they pull up the gangplank. After she misses the pilot boat that could take her to the ship, she hires a helicopter to lower her on to the deck below. Leave it to Lucy to start off a boat trip by air.

First

• First helicopter trip

Lucy Meets Charles Boyer

Filmed January 19, 1956 aired March 5, 1956

Having heard about Lucy's stunts, actor Charles Boyer pretends to be Maurice DuBois when Lucy spots him in a local café. In order to keep her away from Boyer, Ricky pretends to be insanely jealous of the French star. To prove her loyalty to Ricky, Lucy asks Dubois to pretend to be Boyer so she can pretend to be uninterested. Ricky tells the truth after all the antics, and Lucy is so star struck she ruins the man's coat, shirt, and hat. All in a day's work!

Return Home from Europe

Filmed April 5, 1956, aired May 14, 1956

When a job offer means Ricky needs to fly home suddenly, Lucy is upset that she can't take her twenty-five-pound gift of cheese for Mother. Assuming a baby flies for free, she dresses up the cheese to look like an infant, complete with bonnet. When she discovers she will have to pay for her "baby," she and Ethel eat as much of the cheese as they can, and hide the rest in Ricky's band instruments. Chaos ensues when she is accused of getting rid of her baby and gets hauled into the Customs Office for questioning.

Ricky Ricardo-ism

"I am not the father of that chis!"

First

• First airplane trip

Little Ricky Gets a Dog

Filmed November 8, 1956, aired January 21, 1957

The Ricardos' home has turned into a zoo due to Little Ricky's menagerie of animals. When he brings home a puppy, everyone says enough. Fred tells Lucy she has to get rid of the pooch due to the "no pets" clause in their lease, but Little Ricky names his dog after his godfather, and Fred doesn't have the heart to send the puppy packing. A new building tenant does not take kindly to the puppy's barking habits, though, and Fred is forced to choose between the dog and the paying boarder.

Lucy Wants to Move to the Country

Filmed December 6, 1956, aired January 28, 1957

After visiting friends in Connecticut, Lucy decides she wants to quit the city life. She campaigns to convince Ricky to buy a beautiful old colonial home in Westport, but Ricky has already put a deposit down as a gift to his wife. Lucy then decides she can't leave her best friends, so she and the Mertzes dress up like gangsters to convince the homeowners they're not respectable. Once she gets another look at the house, Lucy wants it after all, but the price has just gone up!

Ricky Ricardo-ism

"I assure you, if we could just be alone for a minute, I could 'splain if I could just get a worch in etch wise."

First

• First mention of Lucy wanting to move to Connecticut

✳ Sneaky Tricks ✳

The Séance

Filmed October 19, 1951, aired November 26, 1951

Lucy's new hobby is dabbling in numerology and astrology. She is suddenly seized with the need to have numbers and predictions rule her life. On the day that producer Mr.

Merriweather calls to offer Ricky a job, Lucy tells him "no" because it's a day for Geminis to say no to everything. Ricky is furious, but when Lucy finds out Mr. Merriweather is a fan of the paranormal, too, she and the Mertzes plan a little séance for the producer and his beloved dog, Tillie.

Ricky Ricardo-ism

"Lucy, dun't you like the way I vibrate?"

The Young Fans

Filmed January 18, 1952, aired February 25, 1952

A local teenager named Peggy has a huge crush on Ricky, and thinks he's the living end. She keeps popping in unannounced, and while Lucy is patient at first, she begins to grow a little weary of the young girl's romantic notions about her husband. When Peggy's classmate, Arthur, falls in love with Lucy, the Ricardos come up with a plan to show the two teenagers what it would be like to be married to very elderly people.

The Gossip

Filmed February 15, 1952, aired March 24, 1952

Ricky is exasperated with Lucy's constant gossiping. After arguing about it with Fred and Ethel, the foursome makes a bet about who can go longer without spreading gossip. At first, Lucy and Ethel are very good about not blabbing, but when Ricky and Fred plant a false rumor about a neighbor, the girls can't contain their chatty ways. When the ladies find out the gossip was fake, they turn the tables on their hubbies and end up winning the bet.

Ricky Ricardo-ism

"Birds of a feather smell the same."

Firsts

• First mention of neighbor Grace Foster
• First time Fred mentions his hometown, Steubenville, Ohio

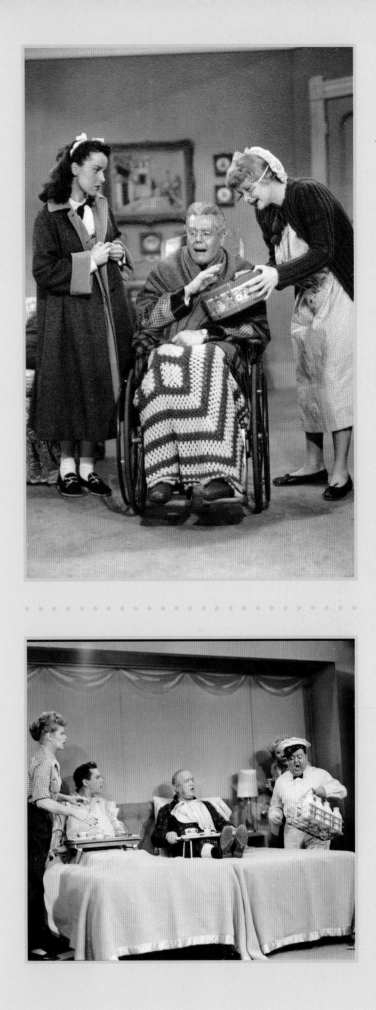

The Camping Trip

Filmed May 8, 1953, aired June 8, 1953

Lucy decides she wants to join Ricky on his "boys weekend," but Ricky doesn't want her anywhere near his males-only camping and fishing trip. Ricky decides to show Lucy how tough an outdoor adventure can be, so he plans a very difficult trip for his wife. Lucy fights back, and with Ethel's help, manages to beat Ricky at his own game. He is confused by her seeming ability to do everything right, until she shoots an already plucked duck (which Ethel has picked up at the market) out of the sky.

Firsts

• First mention of Fred's brother
• First time Ethel drives a car

Lucy Hires an English Tutor

Filmed October 24, 1952, aired December 29, 1952

Lucy is determined that her baby will grow up surrounded by people who speak only the King's English. When she determines that the foursome has much to learn about proper speech, she hires an English tutor. Mr. Livermore does not charge a fee, but he does have a price—he wants to perform his "dippy" song for Ricky. Not wanting to sit through the boring lessons, Ricky secretly agrees to allow Mr. Livermore to perform at the club if he will stop the lessons altogether.

Ricky Ricardo-ism

"I had enough trouble learning how to speak American."

Lucy and Ethel Buy the Same Dress

Filmed September 17, 1953, aired October 19, 1953

The girl's club has a spot on a TV show, so Lucy and Ethel team up to perform the Cole Porter duet, "Friendship." Their rehearsals go well, and they are really cute in the number, but when they decide to wear formal dresses it all goes awry. Each buys the same dress, and each agrees to take her dress back, but when neither of them actually does, they appear on stage as twins, but soon do their best to rip each other's dress to shreds—all in the name of friendship.

Sentimental Anniversary

Filmed December 17, 1953, aired February 1, 1954

All Lucy wants to do on her thirteenth wedding anniversary is stay home and have a romantic dinner with Ricky. Unfortunately for her, the Mertzes have planned a surprise party for the happy couple. To throw everyone off track, Lucy and Ricky pretend to go to a dinner meeting, and then they sneak back to their apartment for some alone time. Meanwhile, the Mertzes come over with cake and gifts, and the Ricardos are forced to hide in the closet while the guests arrive.

Ricky Minds the Baby

Filmed December 3, 1953, aired January 18, 1954

The Tropicana is being painted, so Ricky has a whole week off. Lucy is thrilled, and Ricky is excited about spending time with his family. When the gals go off shopping and leave the toddler with Ricky and Fred, Lucy is weepy and nervous. When Little Ricky wanders down the hallways while daddy and Uncle Fred are watching the fights, Lucy tricks Ricky into thinking the boy is missing! Fred finds his godson and sneaks him into his crib, everyone is confused.

Ricky's Hawaiian Vacation

Filmed February 11, 1954, aired March 22, 1954

Ricky is taking his band to Hawaii and everyone wants to wave *aloha* to the island. When Ricky informs Lucy that he can't afford to take her along, she and the Mertzes scheme to win a Hawaiian trip by doing a stunt on the TV Show *Be a Good Neighbor*. Lucy pretends to do a good deed for their wonderful friends who take care of their elderly mother. Unfortunately for the trio, Ricky is not so inclined to be a great neighbor, and he spoils things for them.

Lucy Cries Wolf

Filmed June 3, 1954, aired October 18, 1954

Lucy reads about a couple who was recently robbed, and she wants to see how Ricky would react if she were in trouble. She calls Ricky and tells him there is a thief, but instead of rushing home, he calls Ethel. Lucy continues to try to trick Ricky into thinking she is in mortal danger, even crawling out the window and onto a ledge to hide. Finally Ricky grows sick of her shenanigans and as she is sulking out in the hallway two robbers grab her and tie her up.

Ricky Ricardo-isms

"Why is it that the news always looks grinner at the other side of the breakfast table?"

"I don't know whether something's really happened to her, or maybe she's just jelling tiger."

The Fashion Show

Filmed December 23, 1954, aired February 28, 1955

Lucy is just dying for a Don Loper dress, so she cons Ricky into letting her spend $100. While at the salon, she overhears talk of a fashion show put on by the wives of Hollywood stars, and she makes it clear that being Ricky Ricardo's wife, she is one of them. When it turns out her dress costs $500, Lucy schemes to get sunburned so Ricky will feel sorry for her. She stays in the sun much too long though, and when Loper asks her to wear a wool suit in the fashion show, Lucy's sneaky ways are painfully clear.

Ricky Ricardo-ism

"You always get burned with your fur skin."

Bull Fight Dance

Filmed February 17, 1955, aired March 28, 1955

Photoplay magazine has asked Lucy to write an article about what it's like being married to Ricky. Lucy uses her answers to blackmail Ricky when she wants a part in his TV benefit show. At first Ricky refuses to let her join in, then he can't find a part for her because she lacks training. He finally figures out a role for her but she's not thrilled. She plays the part of the bull in Ricky's matador number, but she

changes the bull's look and personality, and ends up stealing the show.

Ricky Ricardo-isms

"You just haven't got enough 'sperience."

"Blackmailers can't be shoosers."

Second Honeymoon

Filmed December 8, 1955, aired January 23, 1956

Fred and Ethel are acting like newlyweds on their second honeymoon cruise, but Lucy feels like a third wheel because Ricky has only moments to spend with her. She has no one to talk to, play games with, dance with, or gaze at the moon with. In desperation, she decides to lock herself and Ricky inside their cabin one night so he can't play with the band. When she finds out he has the night off, she calls through the porthole to get Ethel to open the door, but she gets stuck halfway out.

Lucy Gets a Paris Gown

Filmed February 16, 1956, aired March 19, 1956

Lucy is so determined to have an original Jacques Marcel gown that she is willing to starve for it. When Ricky says she can't have one, she vows she will not eat until he changes his mind. With Ethel's help she appears to keep her vow while chowing down behind Ricky's back. When Ricky discovers her ruse he pays her back by sewing Marcel labels into dresses designed by a local tailor and made of sack material. The joke is on him when they become *haute couture*.

Lucy Gets Homesick in Italy

Filmed March 1, 1956, aired April 9, 1956

Frugal Freddie has booked the gang into an Italian hotel that leaves much to be desired—there is no working elevator and no phone in the rooms. Lucy wants to call Little Ricky on his birthday but she has to go up and down many flights of stairs while waiting for the call. Meanwhile, she meets a shoeshine boy who tricks her into believing that it's his birthday, so she throws a party for him and his friends. When her call finally comes through, the children serenade Little Ricky in Italian.

Desert Island

Filmed October 4, 1956, aired November 26, 1956

The fellas are set to judge a bathing beauty contest, and Lucy intends to put a stop to their ogling. She schemes to thwart them by going out on a boat and running out of gasoline. She plans to have their boat's gas tank filled only halfway so they miss the contest, at which point she will "find" a spare thermos filled with gasoline. Her plan goes well until she discovers the spare thermos didn't make it on board, and they are really stranded.

Building a Barbecue

Filmed March 14, 1957, aired April 8, 1957

With Ricky home on vacation, Lucy comes up with a way to trick him into getting out of her hair. She and Ethel pretend they are going to build a barbecue. On cue, Ricky and Fred step in to do the work. Lucy discovers she has lost her wedding ring, and concludes it fell into the cement. That night she takes the barbecue apart looking for her jewelry, to no avail. When Ricky and Fred discover the mess she left they are horrified, but she later finds her ring in a hamburger.

Ricky Ricardo-ism

"Wha' happun?"

Lucy Thinks Ricky is Trying to Murder Her

Filmed September 8, 1951, aired November 5, 1951

Lucy is deeply involved in reading a murder mystery novel called *The Mockingbird Mystery*, so when she hears Ricky on the phone saying he needs to get rid of someone and replace her, she thinks he is talking about her! With Ethel's help, Lucy comes up with a plan to spoil Ricky's plan but she thinks he's succeeded when she takes a drink that has a sleeping medication in it! Later she runs down to the club to confront Ricky and finds him with all his new females—a dog act!

Firsts

• First time Lucy cries—waaaaaaaaah!

• First time we see Lucy and Ricky in pajamas

• First time Lucy mentions that Ethel is her best friend

Drafted

Filmed November 2, 1951, aired December 24, 1951

When a letter comes from the War Department telling Ricky to report to Fort Dix, Lucy thinks the worst—her husband's been drafted! And when Ricky says Fred is going with him, the gals prepare for their soldiers to ship out. They spend their time crying and knitting socks, which leads the men to think their wives are going to have babies! The confusion abounds as the men plan baby showers and the women plan *bon voyage* parties before everyone realizes the truth.

First

• First reference to Lucy's bad singing voice

Lucy is Jealous of Girl Singer

Filmed November 16, 1951, aired December 17, 1951

A gossip columnist indicates that Ricky might be involved in some hanky-panky on the side, and the green-eyed

monster bites Lucy. When she finds a piece of black lace in Ricky's pocket, her suspicions are confirmed, or so she thinks. She nabs a spot in the chorus line at the club in order to have a bird's-eye view of Ricky and the new dancer in his act. When she wrecks the routine with her less-than-stellar dancing, Ricky is not amused.

Ricky Ricardo-ism

"Lucy, if you'll just give me a chance to 'splain."

First

• First time we see the Ricky Ricardo and Orchestra marquee

New Neighbors

Filmed January 25, 1952, aired March 3, 1952

New tenants have arrived in the building, and Lucy and Ethel are curious about who they are. They sneak down to the apartment when the couple is out, and snoop around. When Lucy is caught, she hides in the closet and hears the couple rehearsing for a play. She concludes that they are foreign spies out to infiltrate the government, so the gang springs into action. They call the police and end up firing at the officer who comes to the door—and they end up in the clink.

First

• First time the gang lands in jail

The Kleptomaniac

Filmed March 7, 1952, aired April 14, 1952

Although she has promised Ricky that she won't be involved in any more causes, Lucy finds herself collecting for a charity event. When Ricky finds a wad of cash in her purse and a ton of donated items in the closet, he concludes that his wife is a kleptomaniac. He asks a psychiatrist to evaluate her, but Lucy is wise to his plan and makes one of her own—she will show him just how right he is by pretending to be a bank robber who steals circus elephants on the side.

The Anniversary Present

Filmed May 9, 1952, aired September 9, 1952

Lucy does her best to remind Ricky that their wedding an-

niversary is coming up, but he seems completely disinterested. She doesn't know that he's asked neighbor Grace Foster to help him choose a strand of pearls as a gift. Lucy thinks Ricky is having a love affair with Grace, and when she and Ethel listen in through the furnace pipe, her fears are confirmed (or so she thinks.) She has to see it for herself, so she and Ethel climb out on the scaffolding and pretend to be painters so she can peer through the window.

The Inferiority Complex

Filmed September 6, 1952, aired February 2, 1953

Lucy is convinced she will never amount to anything. Everything she does is a failure and a flop—she can't even salt eggs right. Ricky consults with a psychiatrist who comes to the house pretending to be Ricky's friend. He flirts with Lucy and soothes her ego, but a jealous Ricky soon tosses him out. Now it's up to Ricky and the Mertzes to persuade Lucy she is a talented singer, joke teller, and card player.

Ricky Ricardo-ism

[Looking in phone book] "Physiakiatrist . . . F. . ."

The Black Eye

Filmed September 19, 1952, aired March 9, 1953

Lucy and Ricky are reading a murder mystery when they are overheard by the busybody Mertzes, who deduce that Lucy is being abused. When Lucy is seen sporting a black eye, Fred tries to help by sending her flowers from Ricky, but he signs his own name, and when Ethel finds out she socks Fred in the eye. Fred then hits Ricky for starting the whole thing. The only one without a black eye is Ethel, but she ends up with one when she is hit in the face with a book.

Ricky Ricardo-ism

"Wha' happun'?"

Firsts

• First time Lucy wears maternity clothing (five months pregnant)
• First time Ricky asks, "Wha' happun'?"

Pregnant Women Are Unpredictable

Filmed October 10, 1952, aired December 15, 1952

Lucy and Ricky can't decide on names for their baby. Should it be Pamela and Scott? Juliet and Romeo? Mary and John? Unique and Euphonious? Later, when Ricky brings gifts home for Lucy, they all turn out to be gifts for the baby, and Lucy is beginning to think Ricky doesn't love her. Ethel tells Ricky he should take the mommy-to-be out for an evening of dinner and dancing, but when he does Lucy cries that he doesn't care about the baby!

Lucy's Last Birthday

Filmed April 10, 1953, aired May 11, 1953

Poor Lucy, she thinks all her loved ones have forgotten her special day. Ethel doesn't mention anything, and there is no gift from Ricky. When Mrs. Trumble catches her weeping, she throws a little party for the two of them, but Lucy leaves in tears to walk in the park. She meets up with a group called "The Friends of the Friendless," who accompany her to the Tropicana where she intends to confront Ricky, but instead finds there is a party waiting for her.

First

• First birthday celebration (Lucy's)

Lucy is Matchmaker

Filmed April 25, 1953, aired May 25, 1953

Fred's bachelor pal Eddie Grant is in town on business, and Lucy is determined to set him up with one of her friends. Lucy tells Eddie all about Sylvia, but Eddie is convinced that Lucy is Sylvia, and when Sylvia can't make the date at the last minute, Lucy goes to Eddie's hotel to tell him. In typical fashion, Ricky and Fred show up at the hotel to have lunch with Eddie only to find their wives in Eddie's room trying on the lingerie that Eddie promised to sell them, wholesale.

Ricky Ricardo-isms

"They have a whole other face underneath the face you marry."

"I thought I tol' you to mess out."

"You never do what I tol' you!"

Too Many Crooks

Filmed October 29, 1953, aired November 30, 1953

There is a thief named Madame X roaming the neighborhood, and everyone is on edge. When Lucy is seen sneaking out of the Mertzes' apartment with one of Fred's suits, Ethel suspects her best friend. And when Lucy spots Ethel out on her fire escape, Lucy's mind whirls with wrong conclusions. In order to catch her friend in the act, Lucy tells Ethel she is going out, but hides in her apartment hoping to stop Ethel's crime spree. Instead, Lucy ends up catching the real crook!

Ricky's Old Girl Friend

Filmed November 19, 1953, aired December 21, 1953

Lucy and Ricky take a quiz about marriage and discuss past loves. When he can't think of any, Ricky makes up the name Carlotta Romero, and the next day when Lucy reads in the paper that Carlotta is in town, she has nightmares about her husband leaving her for the beautiful *señorita*. It turns out that Ricky did work with Carlotta years ago, when she was a little girl, but when she shows up at the apartment to meet with him, Lucy is happy to see she's grown up—and filled out.

First

• First dream sequence

Fan Magazine Interview

Filmed January 7, 1954, aired February 8, 1954

Ricky's agent has arranged for a newspaper reporter to spend the day with Lucy and Ricky, interviewing them for an article on a happily married couple. The Ricardos ham it up, pretending to be newlyweds without a care in the world. When Lucy finds a postcard in Ricky's pocket inviting a woman for a date at the club, she goes to visit her competition, an old, frumpy woman, and Lucy is confused. It turns out the postcard was a publicity stunt set up by Ricky's agent.

Oil Wells

Filmed January 14, 1954, aired February 15, 1954

The gang buys some oil stock from a new tenant, who promises them a big payoff any day. When a detective pal of Fred's stops by asking about the oilman from Texas, Lucy immediately decides that the police are looking for him because he's a swindler. To everyone's relief, Lucy and Ethel succeed in selling their stock back. Later Fred's pal drops by again, this time to call his wife to tell her he just bought some oil stock, moments before they hit a gusher—they're rich!

Ricky Ricardo-isms

"Do you think that I'm gonna buy oil stock from a perfectly stranger?"

"Yeah, Fred, what's five shares to a big oil typhoon like you?"

"Never cross your chickens before your bridges is hatched."

California, Here We Come!

Filmed November 4, 1954, aired January 10, 1955

Lucy gets a letter from her mother informing Lucy that she plans to go to California with them! This news makes Ricky

crazy, and he starts yelling about how everyone is butting in on their trip. Fred and Ethel overhear and think they are not wanted, and a fight ensues. They straighten everything out, but then they find the women have packed so much stuff they can't possibly take it all, so they decide to ship everything and have Mother and Little Ricky fly out later.

Ricky Ricardo-ism

"Well, we'll have to live it here, that's all!"

First

• First time we met Mother McGillicuddy

Ricky Sells the Car

Filmed September 29, 1955, aired October 24, 1955

Ricky has found a buyer for the Pontiac, so they will take the train back to New York. Along the way, he forgets to buy train tickets for the Mertzes! Lucy gives them her tickets as a show of good faith, but Ricky wants to trade them back because there are no more sleeping compartments left. When Ethel catches Lucy trying to slip the compartment tickets out of the pocket of sleeping Fred's jacket, she thinks Lucy is making hanky-panky with her husband!

Homecoming

Filmed October 13, 1955, aired November 7, 1955

The gang is back from Hollywood, and all the attention is now on Ricky. He can't stand that everyone is treating him like a star, and Lucy can't stand that no one is paying attention to her. When a magazine calls to do an article on Lucy's life as Mrs. Ricardo, the woman tells Lucy that her every waking moment should be dedicated to making Ricky happy. Lucy takes the advice to heart, thinking it'd be what Ricky wants, but all he wants is to go back to the way things used to be.

Lucy's Italian Movie

Filmed March 8, 1956, aired April 16, 1956

While on a train to Rome, Lucy meets up with an Italian movie director who wants her to be in his movie. She learns the film is called *Bitter Grapes*, so assuming it's about the wine industry, she sets out to "soak up a little local color" in a vineyard. She is chosen to crush grapes in a vat and manages to get into a big fight with her stomping partner. Upon her return, she learns her part was to be a typical American tourist, but her purple skin causes her to lose the role to Ethel.

Ricky Ricardo-ism

"Oh no you dun't."

Off to Florida

Filmed September 13, 1956, aired November 12, 1956

Lucy and Ethel are headed to Florida by train to meet the boys who left early to go fishing. At the last minute, Lucy can't find the train tickets so they decide to share a ride with a woman who is also traveling south. When they hear a radio report about an escaped axe murderer and then find a hatchet in the car trunk, they assume their driver is someone to be feared. During a diner stop, the lady drives off without them, and they have to hitch a ride on a poultry truck.

Ricky Ricardo-ism

"There's a couple of thins I'd like you to 'splain."

Lucy Misses the Mertzes

Filmed December 20, 1956, aired February 11, 1957

After exchanging hugs and house keys, the Ricardos are on their way to Connecticut. At first Lucy is thrilled with her new home, but she soon grows bored of the quiet and the lack of friends. She and Ricky decide to go visit the Mertzes at the same time the Mertzes decide to visit them. After missing each other at the train station, Lucy and Ricky go home to bed, but when they hear noises in the house they think it's burglars. Turns out it's just their best pals.

Ricky Ricardo-isms

"Yeah, I'm gonna be a real country square."

"You know, we're gonna be real suburbanitees."

Housewarming

Filmed February 28, 1957, aired April 1, 1957

Lucy's attempt to bring Ethel into her new set of friends falls flat until Ethel and Betty Ramsey realize they were childhood pals. Now Lucy is the one feeling left out as the two Albuquerque girls are suddenly inseparable. When Lucy hears Ethel discussing housewarming gifts, she mistakenly deduces that the neighbors are throwing them a welcome party, so she and Ricky practice being surprised, and then go out for the evening. The surprise is on Lucy when they return to an empty house.

The Quiz Show

Filmed October 5, 1951, aired November 12, 1951

Lucy's accounting practices leave much to be desired, and when Ricky learns her books are off by almost $1,000, he cuts off her spending. Lucy goes on a radio show called *Females are Fabulous*, which offers a big prize for pulling off a stunt. Lucy must pretend that the man who shows up on the doorstep is her long-lost first husband, which is bad enough, but when two men show up, she has to explain how she was married to both of them!

Ricky Ricardo-ism

"I'd like a lohgical 'splanation of this."

Firsts

- First time someone makes fun of Ricky's English
- First time Lucy sings
- First mention of Lucy's problems managing money
- First time Lucy wears polka dots
- First guest performer—Frank Nelson as Freddie Filmore

The Amateur Hour

Filmed December 7, 1951, aired January 14, 1952

Lucy's spending is out of control, so she has to get a job to pay for her clothing purchases. She isn't qualified to do much, but when she finds a babysitting job that pays $5 an hour, she jumps on it. It turns out that the pay is so high because the "baby" is a pair of obnoxious twin boys who do everything but set fire to Lucy. Their mom calls and asks Lucy to take her place in their musical act in a contest, saying she can keep the cash prize if she wins, so Lucy jumps at the opportunity.

The Freezer

Filmed March 21, 1952, aired April 28, 1952

Meat is getting too expensive, so Lucy asks Ricky if they can buy a freezer so they can buy large amounts of meat

less expensively. Ethel wants in too, so when her uncle says he will give them a freezer, the gals mistakenly buy seven hundred pounds of meat! They attempt to sell some of it, and then when the guys arrive home to see the freezer, they hide the beef in the cold furnace, which is an okay idea until the furnace is turned back on and all that meat turns into a massive barbecue!

Firsts

- First mention of address (623 East 68th Street)
- First mention of Ethel's Aunt Em and Uncle Oscar

Sales Resistance

Filmed August 29, 1952, aired January 26, 1953

Lucy is unable to resist a good salesman, and buys a Handy Dandy Kitchen Helper, which is all but useless. Ricky makes her return the gadget, but when she does, she is tricked into buying a vacuum cleaner she can't afford. Knowing that she can't keep it, but afraid to come into contact with the salesman again, Lucy attempts to sell the appliance herself, using the same technique that was used on her. She fails, but so does Ricky when he tries to return it.

The Ricardos Change Apartments

Filmed April 16, 1953, aired May 18, 1953

Now that the baby has been born, Lucy needs more space for all his gear. She longs to have another bedroom for Little Ricky, but big Ricky says they can't afford to move. When

The Operetta

Filmed May 23, 1952, aired October 13, 1952

Club treasurer Lucy has been borrowing from the club's account for two years, and now there is nothing left. She wants to stage a benefit production to raise funds. Because she can't pay the royalty fees, Lucy is forced to write a play herself—*The Pleasant Peasant*—and rent the costumes and set using post-dated checks! Everything is going well until some men appear on stage and start repossessing the scenery. It seems the checks Lucy wrote have bounced!

Lucy learns that another couple needs a smaller place, she asks them to switch apartments, planning to take the extra rent money out of her food budget. She and the Mertzes move all the furniture, unaware that Ricky has hired moving men to do the job, so everything is switched back to where it started!

Ricky Ricardo-ism

"I won' swish apartments."

First

• First time Lucy wants to move to a different apartment

Lucy Wants New Furniture

Filmed May 1, 1953, aired June 1, 1953

Once again, Lucy buys furniture that Ricky tells her they can't afford. Since she can't return it, Ricky keeps the furniture for his office and tells her she is going to have to pay for it out of her allowance. That means no new clothes, and no going to the beauty parlor. When a big social event comes up, Lucy attempts to make her own dress and gives herself a home permanent. Everything turns out so dreadfully that Ricky takes pity on her and gives her the furniture back.

Ricky Ricardo-ism

"Cut down on your 'stravaganzas."

The Girls Go Into Business

Filmed September 11, 1953, aired October 12, 1953

Lucy and Ethel believe that Hansen's Dress Shop is a gold mine, so when it goes up for sale they pounce on it, without the okay of their husbands. When the sales don't come pouring in, they are afraid Ricky and Fred will be furious. Soon they are thrilled to receive an offer to buy their shop for slightly more than they paid for it. Later they learn they could have made a lot more money if they had sold it for tens of thousands of dollars to a man who needed the space to build a skyscraper!

First

• First time Ricky mentions he wants to go into business for himself

The Million-Dollar Idea

Filmed November 28, 1953, aired January 11, 1954

Lucy is overdrawn on her budget again, about twenty-five years into the future. Fred convinces her to sell her delicious salad dressing, so she and Ethel go into business. They go on TV to sell it and the orders come pouring in. When Ricky learns of their scheme, he figures out that they are going to lose money on each jar, so they go on TV again to try to "unsell" it. Unfortunately, their sales technique is even funnier the second time around, and they end up with a ton of orders.

Lucy is Envious

Filmed February 16, 1954, aired March 29, 1954

Lucy's ritzy friend is in town spearheading a charity drive and Lucy doesn't want all her old school chums to know she is not wealthy. She and Ethel both agree to give "five" without realizing that means $500! To earn the money the dynamic duo dresses as "Women from Mars" and climb the Empire State Building to promote a movie. Unfortunately for them, they end up causing mass panic and chaos all over the tri-state area, but at least they earned the money.

Ricky Ricardo-ism

"Lucy, how much did she bit you for?"

The Business Manager

Filmed June 17, 1954, aired October 4, 1954

Lucy's household expenses are out of control so Ricky hires a business manager to handle their personal finances. Mr. Hickox puts the Ricardos on a stringent budget and they are suffering. Lucy begins to shop for her neighbors, collecting cash from them and charging their groceries. Suddenly she is flush with dough and Ricky thinks she is playing the stock market. Ricky buys some stock he thinks Lucy wants, and hits it big, earning enough for Lucy to pay the grocery bill.

First

• First time one of the Lucy's money-making schemes makes money

Lucy Goes to Monte Carlo

Filmed March 29, 1956, aired May 7, 1956

Being in the gambling mecca of the world, Lucy wants to visit the casinos. Ricky doesn't want her anywhere near the blackjack tables, but when she finds a chip on the floor, she places it on the table and wins big. Meanwhile Fred tells Ricky they haven't made any money on the tour so when Ricky finds Lucy's cash stashed in Ethel's suitcase, he thinks Fred is embezzling funds. A huge fight ensues until Lucy confesses, bets all her money, and loses it all.

Lucy Gets Chummy with the Neighbors

Filmed January 10, 1957, aired February 18, 1957

Lucy's new neighbor, Betty Ramsey, has a connection with a local furniture store, and tells Lucy she can get her a discount on all the furniture she will need. Lucy thinks she's within the limits of her $500 budget, but she later learns that she spent almost $3,000 more than Ricky said she could. Needing to return the furniture but not wanting to tell the truth about the money, Lucy starts a fight with the Ramseys that is only stopped when she fesses up about the money.

✳   What a Mess!   ✳

Lucy Writes a Play

Filmed December 22, 1951, aired February 4, 1952

Lucy decides she is going to enter a play in a women's club competition. Hoping Ricky will play the lead, she calls her play *A Tree Grows in Havana*. When Ricky refuses the role, she switches the scene to Jolly Ole England with Fred as the lead male. Ricky learns that a Hollywood producer is going to attend the contest, so he takes over for Fred, but he is unaware the script now calls for a "cheerio" rather than an "ai yi yi," and Lucy's playwriting debut is ruined.

Firsts

- First mention of the Wednesday Afternoon Fine Arts League
- First time Lucy and Ethel attempt to put on a play

Lucy Gets Ricky on the Radio

Filmed April 11, 1951, aired May 19, 1952

When he pretends to know all the answers during a radio quiz game show, Lucy thinks her husband is a genius. She gets them on the show and thinks he will thank her, but he is not thrilled. He tells Lucy she needs to figure out how to keep him from looking like a fool. Lucy goes to the station and steals what she thinks are the answers to the questions, but they turn out not to be, and she and Ricky are the first couple in the show's history to get all three questions wrong.

Ricky Ricardo-ism

"Who do you think you are married to, a country pumpkin?"

Redecorating

Filmed August 15, 1952, aired November 24, 1952

Lucy and Ethel each buy raffle tickets for rooms of new furniture. Ricky has tickets to a show but Lucy won't leave the house until she hears if she's won, so Fred says he will give Lucy a fake call and tell her she's won. Lucy jumps into action, sells her old furniture, and wallpapers her apartment in anticipation. Ricky comes home to a mess and tells Lucy the call was a fake. He buys his old furniture back at a ridiculous price, but it turns out that Lucy won the contest after all!

Ricky Ricardo-ism

"Now wait a minute, don't hurry up so fast!"

Firsts

• First time Lucille Ball attempts to hide her pregnancy (four months pregnant)
• First time Lucy asks for new furniture

Baby Pictures

Filmed October 1, 1953, aired November 2, 1953

Lucy is sick of the Applebys bragging about their little boy, but she tries really hard not to be a boasting mama herself. The day after the Applebys are at their home, Lucy drops in unexpectedly on Carolyn, and insults her and her son, Stevie. The ensuing fight causes Charlie Appleby to cancel Ricky's appearance at his TV studio, so Lucy has to eat crow and figure out a way to fix the problem she's caused. She does so by bringing Little Stevie on the show as the cutest baby.

Redecorating the Mertzes' Apartment

Filmed October 22, 1953, aired Novmber 23, 1953

Ethel keeps asking Lucy if the club meetings can be held at the Ricardos' because she is ashamed of the look of her apartment. Lucy thinks she and Ricky should help their dear friends, so they throw them a painting and redecorating party. With the walls still wet, Lucy removes the feathers from Fred's chair just as he turns on a fan! The result is a feathery disaster, and Lucy is forced to give Ethel and Fred her practically brand new furniture to make up for the things she ruined.

Ricky Ricardo-ism

"Well, I did told you so!"

Bonus Bucks

Filmed February 4, 1954, aired March 8, 1954

A newspaper contest has everyone in town comparing serial numbers on dollar bills. Ricky finds a $300 winner and hides it in Lucy's purse for her to find, but she gives it to the grocery boy who gives it to Ethel in change. They rip the bill in half and decide to split the winnings. Lucy's half of the dollar mistakenly goes to the laundry and she ends up in the starch vat! After they pay for the cabs and the bill to fix what she broke at the laundry, there is only $1 of prize money left.

Tennessee Ernie Visits

Filmed April 1, 1954, aired May 3, 1954

When Lucy's mother's friend's roommate's cousin's middle boy from Bent Fork, Tennessee comes a-callin', the Ricardos' lives are put into uproar. Ernie sleeps in the living room, sings at 6AM, and eats everything he can put in his mouth. To get him to skeedadle, Lucy dresses up as a "wicked city woman" and attempts to "vamp" him, but it turns out he likes it! Now that he's tasted city life, they fear he will become the houseguest who never leaves.

Ricky Ricardo-ism

"Well I'll be ding-donged."

First

• First overnight guest at the Ricardos' (Cousin Ernie) besides Fred or Ethel

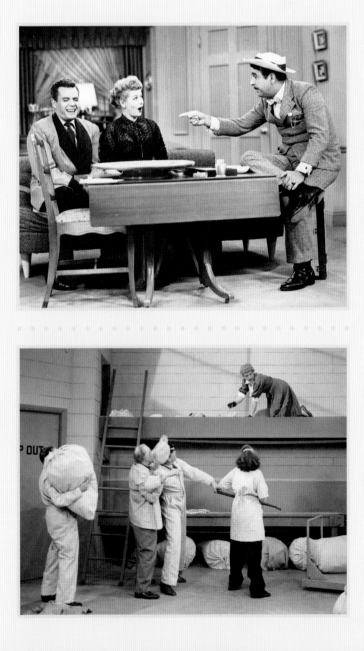

Mr. and Mrs. TV Show

Filmed June 24, 1954, aired November 1, 1954/April 11, 1955

Lucy is out to lunch when she meets an advertising executive. She tells him about her brilliant husband and gets him a job hosting a new TV show. She wants to be on the show too, but Ricky says no until the sponsor insists. Lucy is thrilled to be on TV until she learns that her role was not Ricky's idea, so she plans to teach him a lesson by completely messing up the dress rehearsal. The joke is on her though when it turns out the rehearsal is actually the live show!

Getting Ready

Filmed October 21, 1954, aired December 13, 1954

The Ricardos are traveling to California by car, and the Mertzes will go, too. Fred has a pal in the used car business, so he goes to see what he can find, but when he comes home with a $300 antique jalopy no one can believe it. Ricky tells Fred to return the wreck and get his money back, and to help him they call and pretend to be looking for a car just like the one Fred bought. Instead of getting his money back though, Fred decides to sell the car to the guy who called—Ricky!

Ricky Ricardo-isms

"Who said nothin' about a Cadillac convertible?"

"Well, I think that this time I'm a tighter skate than Fred . . . my flint is skinnier than his?"

Lucy Learns to Drive

Filmed October 28 1954, aired January 3, 1955

Ricky has bought a brand-new Pontiac convertible to replace Fred's disaster. Lucy wants to learn to drive, and Ricky tries to teach her, but it goes badly. Later Lucy says she will teach Ethel to drive, and since the keys are in the ignition, Ethel starts the Pontiac up and rams into the Cadillac! Lucy leaves for the auto shop driving the Cadillac and towing the Pontiac, but returns driving the Pontiac and pulling the Cadillac. Luckily for Lucy, Ricky called for insurance already!

Ricky Ricardo-ism

"I'll titch you."

First

• First time Lucy drives a car

First Stop

Filmed November 11, 1954, aired January 17, 1955

On their way west, the gang stops for dinner at a roadside diner. All they can get are stale cheese sandwiches, but they are too tired to keep driving so they decide to spend the night in an ancient dilapidated cabin. Not only are the sleeping accommodations horrible, but a train rumbles by every five minutes, causing a minor earthquake each time. In desperation, they try to sneak away without paying, but find the owner has stolen their steering wheel, which he offers to sell back to them.

L.A. at Last!

Filmed December 2, 1954, aired February 7, 1955

The gang has finally arrived in Hollywood, and Ricky immediately runs off to the studio, so Lucy and the Mertzes decide to go to the Brown Derby. Once inside, Lucy does her best to make a pest of herself with Bill Holden, even managing to make a waiter spill a tray of food on him. Later, Ricky brings Bill home to meet Lucy, so she has to disguise herself with a fake nose so he won't recognize her. In the end he does, but he doesn't squeal to Ricky.

Firsts

• First time we see Hollywood

• First Hollywood star appears (William Holden)

Ricky Needs an Agent

Filmed April 7, 1955, aired May 16, 1955

Lucy thinks it's ridiculous that Ricky is running around opening supermarkets and judging contests. He needs a real agent to go to Metro and demand they put him in a movie—and the redhead is just the girl to do it. Pretending to be Ricky's agent, she storms Walter Reilly's office and demands they put Ricky in a movie, or he will have to leave to take a Broadway role. When Reilly lets Ricky go, Lucy needs to think mighty fast to get his job back.

Lucy and John Wayne

Filmed September 15, 1955, aired October 10, 1955

The police are looking for the two women who stole John Wayne's footprints from Grauman's, so Ricky calls the manager and confesses. He is told to return the prints and no charges will be pressed. The problem is, the cement block is broken. Ricky calls the Duke himself, and John is kind enough to make another one. Through a series of mishaps and misfortunes, it turns out he has to make four more blocks before they get one that sticks. At least he knows who his biggest fan is!

The Great Train Robbery

Filmed October 6, 1955, aired October 31, 1955

All aboard for New York! As usual when Lucy's around, chaos ensues. First she leaves her purse with the tickets in it at the station. Then Mother and Little Ricky have to move compartments and she can't find them. Finally, she hears about a jewel thief on the train, but she mistakes the thief for a detective, and the detective for the thief! Before they've even left the state of California, Lucy has pulled the train's emergency brake four times, and become a legend.

First

• First train trip

The Passports

Filmed November 17, 1955, aired December 19, 1955

Lucy searches for her birth certificate in order to get a passport to travel to Europe. She can't find it, so she calls Jamestown, New York and finds there is no evidence of her being born there. She finds a former babysitter who suddenly claims to be younger than Lucy. She then gets herself locked in a steamer trunk when her old pediatrician stops by, and can't prove who she is! Finally, Mother comes through in a letter complete with birth certificate, from WEST Jamestown!

Staten Island Ferry

Filmed November 24, 1955, aired January 2, 1956

The gang needs new passports and time is running out. At the same time, Fred declares he can't go on the trip because he gets seasick. Lucy agrees to take him on the Staten Island Ferry so he can try out some seasick pills, and they will meet up with Ethel and Ricky at the passport office. Once onboard, Lucy starts to feel queasy herself, so she takes some of Fred's pills and they both fall asleep. They wake up woozy with only minutes to spare before the passport office closes.

First

• First boat trip

Paris at Last!

Filmed January 12, 1956, aired February 27, 1956

The gang has landed in France, and Lucy is determined to act like a native. She sets off to exchange her American money for French, but meets up with a counterfeiter who gives her bad cash. She then orders *escargot* from a local café, can't bear to eat it, and ends up being hauled off to the *bastille* when she pays with phony *francs*. At the jail, she has to have her story translated into Spanish, German, and French in order to be understood. *Vive la France*!

Lucy in the Swiss Alps

Filmed February 23, 1956, aired March 26, 1956

Fred has sent Ricky's band to the wrong Swiss city, and Ricky is worried that he will have to substitute a local oom-pa group for his rumba band. Attempting to get Ricky's mind off his troubles, the gang takes him hiking in the Alps. After a nice climb and a delicious lunch, they head back down but stop in a cabin right before an avalanche. Fearing they might never be rescued, they make confessions and prepare for the worst, but are happily saved by the oom-pa band.

Lucy and the Loving Cup

Filmed November 1, 1956, aired January 7, 1957

Ricky is hosting a celebration for "winningest jockey" Johnny Longden. When Ricky insults Lucy's new hat, she jokes that she will wear Johnny's trophy on her head. She puts it on as a joke but then can't get it off. She needs to go to a silversmith to have it removed, so Ethel takes her on the subway, but the two get separated and Lucy is lost under the streets of New York. She tries her best to get someone to help her, but ends up at the celebration still wearing the trophy.

First

• First subway trip

Lucy's Bicycle Trip

Filmed March 22, 1956, aired April 23, 1956

Lucy wants to see more of the countryside, so the gang sets off toward Italy on bicycles. After spending the night in a barn, they are ready to cross the border but Lucy can't find her passport. Ricky and Fred go to the hotel to retrieve it while Lucy stays in France. She tries everything to get to the Italian side, including pretending to be part of a bike race. When Ricky can't find the passport, she realizes it's in her bag, which is already on the Italian side of the border!

First

• First bicycle trip

The Ricardos Visit Cuba

Filmed October 18, 1956, aired December 3, 1956

It's Lucy's first trip to her hubby's native land, and she is nervous about meeting his family. Her worst fears come true when she messes up continually with patriarch Uncle Alberto. Determined to get on his good side, she sets out to buy the cigars he loves but ends up getting accused of theft, and then has to pretend to be a cigar roller when Uncle Alberto walks into the shop. All is well when Little Ricky brings down the house when he performs "Babalu" with his dad.

Lucy Hates to Leave

Filmed December 13, 1956, aired February 4, 1957

Lucy and Ricky are nervous about becoming first-time homeowners. Fred brings a newlywed couple to see their apartment, and they want not only the apartment but the Ricardos' furniture. Lucy decides to sell it to them, but piece by piece buys it all back. The couple wants to move in right away so the Ricardos, Fred the dog, and all their furniture move in with the Mertzes for a couple of days, until Ricky discovers there is a problem and they have to stay for two weeks!

Ricky Ricardo-ism

"Alright, start 'splainin'."

Lucy Raises Chickens

Filmed January 17, 1957, aired March 4, 1957

Country life is proving to be pretty pricey for the Ricardos, so they decide to take on a side business to help defray costs. They settle on an egg business, and when Fred lets on that he used to live on a farm, he and Ricky form a partnership, and the Mertzes move into the guesthouse. When Lucy and Ethel bring home five hundred baby chickens to an ice cold chicken coop, Fred makes them bring the chicks into the house, where Little Ricky lets them loose to run amuck.

Ricky Ricardo-ism

"Lucy, we can't pay our bills by spinning them around on a lousy Susan."

Firsts

- First mention of Ethel and Fred wanting to move to Connecticut
- First time we learn Fred was raised on a farm

Lucy Does the Tango

Filmed February 7, 1957, aired March 11, 1957

Ricky is almost at the end of his rope waiting for his chickens to start laying eggs. He gives them one more day before he gets out of business, which would mean Fred and Ethel would have to move back to the city. Lucy and Ethel

decide to help their cause by buying several dozen eggs and placing them in the hen house. They are on their way to hide the eggs when Ricky tells Lucy he wants to practice their tango routine—complete with "big finish"—while the eggs are in her blouse.

Lucy's Night in Town

Filmed February 21, 1957, aired March 25, 1957

Lucy and Ethel are excited to be seeing a new Broadway musical, until Lucy realizes she had tickets for the matinee! They can only buy two more tickets, so the gals watch the first half. They notice a pair of unoccupied seats so they sneak in for the second half. Lucy knocks Ethel's purse off the balcony and gets it mixed up with that of another lady. An argument ensues, and the manager discovers their lack of tickets, so he makes them pay for two more seats—just as the curtain comes down.

Ricky Ricardo-ism

"Well, swallow it now and chew it later."

First

• First Broadway play

Lucy Raises Tulips

Filmed March 28, 1957, aired April 29, 1957

Lucy has decided to enter her prize tulips in the local garden contest. She asks Ricky to make sure he mows the lawn, but when he fails to finish on time, Lucy jumps on the mower and cannot stop. She runs amuck all over town, including riding over Betty's flowers! She replaces them with waxed blooms and hopes for the best. Meanwhile, Ricky attempts to mow their yard in the dark and does the same thing to Lucy's garden. Both ladies are disqualified when their blooms melt in the hot sun.

First

• First time we see Lucy gardening

Mertz and Kurtz

Filmed July 1, 1954, aired October 11, 1954

Fred's old vaudeville partner, Barney Kurtz, is traveling through town on his tour, so he drops in to visit Fred. Fred has been fibbing for years to his friend that he's a real estate mogul, so Ethel borrows Lucy's nice serving pieces—and then she borrows Lucy to act as her maid, Bessie. Lucy is a bad maid, and it turns out that Barney has been lying, too, to make his grandson proud. The gang feels sorry for Barney so they star him in a show at the club, and invite his family to watch.

Lucy Goes to Scotland

Filmed January 6, 1956, aired February 20, 1956

In her dream, Lucy returns to the place her McGillicuddy ancestors called home—Kildoonan, Scotland. She dreams that she happens upon this lovely village at a time they are most in need. She is thrilled at their reception when they find out her family name. The trouble is they need her so they can throw her to the two-headed dragon! Guarded by Scotty MacTavish MacDougal McArdo, Lucy tries to be a good sport, but luckily wakes up before she meets her doom.

Lucy and Bob Hope

Filmed June 5, 1956, aired October 1, 1956

Lucy thinks she is helping Ricky by trying to get Bob Hope to perform at the opening of his new Club Babalu. She meets the popular comedian at a ballgame, where she pretends to be a hot dog vendor and a pitcher, all of which ends up with Bob getting bopped on the head with a baseball. When Lucy tells Bob she is really talented, he tells Ricky he won't do the show without her. The trio ends up doing a baseball number and Lucy's spikes get caught in the new floor tiles.

Little Ricky Gets Stage Fright

Filmed June 21, 1956, aired October 22, 1956

Little Ricky has a meltdown when he has to perform in his music school recital. He proclaims that he doesn't want to play the drums anymore, so the gang tries to persuade him that it's fun to perform in front of a crowd. Ricky agrees to allow his son and his band to perform at the club one night, but when the ukulele player comes down with the measles, Lucy steps in and helps her son get over his stage fright by dressing up in the sick boy's costume and strumming along to the tune.

Visitor from Italy

Filmed September 20, 1956, aired October 29, 1956

Mario Orsatti shows up at the Ricardos' and they can't remember where they met him. With the Mertzes' help, they discover he was their gondolier in Venice, and he is in the U.S. to visit his brother. Lucy thinks his brother has moved to San Francisco, so Mario takes jobs to raise bus fare to cross the country. He is no good working as a bus boy at Ricky's club, but he does well at a job in a pizzeria. When he is unable to work because he has no work permit, Lucy fills in for him and learns to flip dough like a real pizza chef.

Little Ricky's School Pageant

Filmed October 25, 1956, aired December 17, 1956

PTA mom Lucy is helping out with Little Ricky's school play. All the adults are taking roles in the production—Ricky plays a hollow tree, Fred takes the role of Hippity Hoppity the Frog, Ethel is the Fairy Queen, and Lucy lands the plum role of the snaggle-toothed witch. Little Ricky inherits a starring role when another boy drops out, and it takes everyone's help to pull the production off in style.

Lucy and Superman

Filmed November 15, 1956, aired January 14, 1957

Lucy and Carolyn Appleby are arguing about the date of their sons' fifth birthday parties. When Lucy announces that Ricky is going to ask his pal, Superman, to attend Little Ricky's bash, Carolyn agrees to change Stevie's festivities. The problem arises when Superman says he can't make it, so determined Lucy dresses as the Man of Steel so Little Ricky won't be disappointed. Lucy is out on a ledge when the real Superman shows up to surprise the birthday boy.

Ricky Ricardo-isms

"You shouldn't cross your bridges before they're hatched."
"You shouldn't burn your chickens behind you."

Ragtime Band

Filmed February 14, 1957, aired March 18, 1957

Lucy generously offers Ricky's musical services for the Westport Historical Society's annual fundraiser, but Ricky has other ideas. Lucy then decides to form a combo with her son and the Mertzes, but their little quartet is hardly ready for prime time. Ricky is finally persuaded to bring in his band to play a few numbers, and allows Lucy and her group to show off their musical abilities during a south-of-the-border calypso number.

The Ricardos Dedicate a Statue

Filmed April 4, 1957, aired May 6, 1957

As chairperson of the Yankee Doodle Day festivities, Lucy and her pals are all involved in the day's events. Ricky is giving the address, Fred is the town crier, Lucy is in charge, and Ethel is doing all the work. Suddenly Little Ricky's dog runs away and Lucy takes the car to chase after it, forgetting that the new statue that is to be dedicated is also in the driveway. With the sculpture in ruins, Lucy dresses up as a Minuteman and tries to trick the assembled crowd into believing she is made of stone.

"Then how come he hasn't learned to obedience?"

"I am not going to be seen in those silly American snickers."

First

• Desi Arnaz, Jr. makes his *I Love Lucy* debut

✳ The Special Cases ✳

A couple of *I Love Lucy* episodes are so special that they can't be pigeonholed into a specific category. They stand on their own and are unique in the history of this show. Indeed, they are all groundbreaking in their own way. The "pregnancy episodes" were a leap of faith for the show as no one knew how the American public would react to Lucy Ricardo being "in the family way" (even though Lucy and Desi were married in real life and on the show). They were worried that parents would ban the show for outwardly discussing Lucy's condition, and it was during these episodes that the Ricardos' twin beds were permanently pushed apart so as not to give children any funny ideas about married people sharing the same bed.

The Christmas episode was also revolutionary because it was a gift to fans, and it contained actual flashbacks within the episode. The couples actually think back to past events, and the audience gets to relive them on screen. This episode was not originally part of the syndication package because no one believed anyone would want to watch a Christmas episode in April or August. How wrong they were.

Lucy is Enceinte

Filmed October 3, 1952, aired December 18, 1952

Lucy is thrilled to find out a baby is on the way, but when she tries to tell Ricky the blessed news, she keeps getting interrupted by phone calls and nosey neighbors. She then goes to the club to tell him, but can't do it in front of the band. In desperation she attends Ricky's show and slips him a note saying someone in the audience is expecting. Ricky starts to sing the baby a song, and looks around the room for the happy couple until he sees Lucy and realizes—"It's me!"

Lucy Goes to the Hospital

Filmed November 14, 1952, aired January 19, 1953

Lucy announces, "Ricky, this is it" and he and the Mertzes spring into action. Unfortunately, Ethel can't reach the doctor, Fred drops the suitcase, and Ricky almost leaves without his wife. Ricky has to leave to go to the club to perform his new African voodoo number. When Fred calls to say the baby has arrived, Ricky rushes back in full makeup, sending the hospital staff and security into a frenzy. Finally, Ricky is able to take his first look at his son—and he faints.

Ricky Ricardo-ism

"I'm at the hospital in the waiting father's room."

The *I Love Lucy* Christmas Show

Filmed November 22, 1956, aired December 24, 1956

On the Eve of Christmas, Little Ricky is concerned that Santa Claus won't make it down the chimney. Once the boy is in bed, the gang starts trimming the tree and reminiscing about past events. They remember when they found out about Lucy's pregnancy, and when Little Ricky was born. The next morning all the adults dress as Santa to surprise Little Ricky, but when they hide in the kitchen to watch him, they count *five* Clauses. Merry Christmas everybody!

✳ I Love Lucy Credits ✳

Season One (episodes 1-35)

Writers: Bob Carroll, Jr., Jess Oppenheimer, Madelyn Pugh
Executive Producer: Desi Arnaz
Producer: Jess Oppenheimer
Director: Marc Daniels

Season Two (episodes 36-64, 66, 67)

Writers: Bob Carroll, Jr., Jess Oppenheimer, Madelyn Pugh
Executive Producer: Desi Arnaz
Producer: Jess Oppenheimer
Directors: William Asher and Marc Daniels

Season Three (episodes 65, 68-97)

Writers: Bob Carroll, Jr., Jess Oppenheimer, Madelyn Pugh
Executive Producer: Desi Arnaz
Producer: Jess Oppenheimer
Director: William Asher

Season Four (episodes 98-127)

Writers: Bob Carroll, Jr., Jess Oppenheimer, Madelyn Pugh
Executive Producer: Desi Arnaz
Producer: Jess Oppenheimer
Director: William Asher

Season Five (episodes 128-153)

Writers: Bob Carroll, Jr., Jess Oppenheimer, Madelyn Pugh, Bob Schiller, Bob Weiskopf
Executive Producer: Desi Arnaz
Producer: Jess Oppenheimer
Director: James Kern

Season Six (episodes 154-179)

Writers: Bob Carroll, Jr., Madelyn Pugh Martin, Bob Schiller, Bob Weiskopf
Producer: Desi Arnaz
Directors: William Asher and James Kern

Although the most popular sitcom on television for five out of its six seasons, *I Love Lucy* won very few awards from the Academy of Television Arts and Sciences. It won a total of four trophies, including one each for Lucille Ball and Vivian Vance for acting. Interestingly, Desi Arnaz, the brains behind so much of the series, as well as a starring actor and musician—and at times its executive producer, producer, and director—was never nominated.

Wins

- Best Situation Comedy, 1953, 1954
- Best Comedienne, Lucille Ball, 1953
- Best Series Supporting Actress, Vivian Vance, 1954
- Best Actress, Continuing Performance, Lucille Ball, 1956

Nominations

For I Love Lucy

- Best Situation Comedy, 1952
- Best Written Comedy Material, Oppenheimer, Pugh, and Carroll, 1955
- Best Situation Comedy, 1955
- Best Comedy Writing: Oppenheimer, Pugh, and Carroll, 1956

For Lucille Ball

- Best Comedian or Comedienne, 1952
- Most Outstanding Personality, 1953
- Best Female Star of Regular Series, 1954
- Best Actress Starring in a Regular Series, 1955
- Best Comedienne, 1956
- Best Continuing Performance by a Comedienne in a Series, 1957
- Best Continuing Performance (Female) in a Series by a Comedienne, Singer, Hostess, Dancer, M.C., Announcer, Narrator, Panelist, or Any Person Who Essentially Plays Herself, 1958

For Vivian Vance

- Best Supporting Actress in a Regular Series, 1955

- Best Supporting Performance by an Actress, 1957
- Best Continuing Supporting Performance by an Actress in a Television Series, 1958

For William Frawley

- Best Series Supporting Actor, 1954
- Best Supporting Actor in a Regular Series, 1955
- Best Actor in a Supporting Role, 1956

The Nielson ratings are a system of measuring television audiences in order to gauge their size and composition. They measure total audience size (based on percentages) and demographics (age, gender, socioeconomic class, race, and area of the country). *I Love Lucy* had the honor of being in the top three for all its six seasons, and for four of them, it was the number-one show in the country.

Season One 1951–52 (ballet, Vitameatavegamin): Ranked #3

Season Two 1952–53 (chocolate factory, birth of Little Ricky): Ranked #1

Season Three 1953–54 (salad dressing, martians): Ranked #1

Season Four 1954–55 (Hollywood): Ranked #1

Season Five 1955–56 (Europe): Ranked #2

Season Six 1956–57 (move to Connecticut): Ranked #1

Shots of various I Love Lucy sets:

"Lucy Thinks Ricky is Trying to Murder Her"

"The Diner"

"The Ricardos Are Interviewed"

"Lucy Raises Chickens"

"Getting Ready"

"Lucy Raises Chickens"

"Lucy Raises Chickens"

"Lucy Raises Chickens"

Chronological Episode Listing

Season One (1951–1952)

1: Lucy Thinks Ricky is Trying to Murder Her
2: The Girls Want to Go to a Nightclub
3: Be a Pal
4: The Diet
5: The Quiz Show
6: The Audition
7: The Séance
8: Men Are Messy
9: Drafted
10: The Fur Coat
11: Lucy is Jealous of Girl Singer
12: The Adagio
13: The Benefit
14: The Amateur Hour
15: Lucy Plays Cupid
16: Lucy Fakes Illness
17: Lucy Writes a Play
18: Breaking the Lease
19: The Ballet
20: The Young Fans
21: New Neighbors
22: Fred and Ethel Fight
23: The Moustache
24: The Gossip
25: Pioneer Women
26: The Marriage License
27: The Kleptomaniac
28: Cuban Pals
29: The Freezer
30: Lucy Does a Television Commercial
31: The Publicity Agent
32: Lucy Gets Ricky on the Radio
33: Lucy's Schedule
34: Ricky Thinks He's Getting Bald
35: Ricky Asks for a Raise

Season Two (1952–1953)

36: The Anniversary Present
37: The Handcuffs
38: The Operetta
39: Job Switching
40: The Saxophone
41: Vacation from Marriage
42: The Courtroom
43: Redecorating
44: Ricky Loses His Voice
45: Sales Resistance
46: The Inferiority Complex

47: The Club Election
48: The Black Eye
49: Lucy Changes Her Mind
50: Lucy is "Enceinte"
51: Pregnant Women are Unpredictable
52: Lucy's Showbiz Swan Song
53: Lucy Hires an English Tutor
54: Ricky Has Labor Pains
55: Lucy Becomes a Sculptress
56: Lucy Goes to the Hospital
57: No Children Allowed
58: Lucy Hires a Maid
59: The Indian Show
60: Lucy's Last Birthday
61: The Ricardos Change Apartments
62: Lucy is Matchmaker
63: Lucy Wants New Furniture
64: The Camping Trip
66: [sic] Ricky and Fred are TV Fans
67: Never Do Business with Friends

Season Three (1953–1954)

65: [sic] Ricky's LIFE Story
68: The Girls Go Into Business
69: Lucy and Ethel Buy the Same Dress
70: Equal Rights
71: Baby Pictures
72: Lucy Tells the Truth
73: The French Revue
74: Redecorating the Mertzes' Apartment
75: Too Many Crooks
76: Changing the Boys' Wardrobe
77: Lucy Has Her Eyes Examined
78: Ricky's Old Girl Friend
79: The Million-Dollar Idea
80: Ricky Minds the Baby
81: The Charm School
82: Sentimental Anniversary
83: Fan Magazine Interview
84: Oil Wells
85: Ricky Loses His Temper
86: Home Movies
87: Bonus Bucks
88: Ricky's Hawaiian Vacation
89: Lucy is Envious
90: Lucy Writes a Novel
91: Lucy's Club Dance
92: The Diner
93: The Black Wig

94: Tennessee Ernie Visits
95: Tennessee Ernie Hangs On
96: The Golf Game
97: The Sublease

Season Four (1954–1955)

98: Lucy Cries Wolf
99: The Matchmaker
100: The Business Manager
101: Mr. and Mrs. TV Show
102: Mertz and Kurtz
103: Ricky's Movie Offer
104: Ricky's Screen Test
105: Lucy's Mother-in-Law
106: Ethel's Birthday
107: Ricky's Contract
108: Getting Ready
109: Lucy Learns to Drive
110: California, Here We Come!
111: First Stop
112: Tennessee Bound
113: Ethel's Home Town
114: L.A. at Last!
115: Don Juan and the Starlets
116: Lucy Gets in Pictures
117: The Fashion Show
118: The Hedda Hopper Story
119: Don Juan is Shelved
120: Bull Fight Dance
121: Hollywood Anniversary
122: The Star Upstairs
123: In Palm Springs
124: Harpo Marx
125: The Dancing Star
126: Ricky Needs an Agent
127: The Tour

Season Five (1955–1956)

128: Lucy Visits Grauman's
129: Lucy and John Wayne
130: Lucy and the Dummy
131: Ricky Sells the Car
132: The Great Train Robbery
133: The Homecoming
134: The Ricardos Are Interviewed
135: Lucy Goes to a Rodeo
136: Nursery School
137: Ricky's European Booking
138: The Passports
139: Staten Island Ferry
140: Bon Voyage
141: Second Honeymoon
142: Lucy Meets the Queen
143: The Fox Hunt

144: Lucy Goes to Scotland
145: Paris at Last!
146: Lucy Meets Charles Boyer
147: Lucy Gets a Paris Gown
148: Lucy in the Swiss Alps
149: Lucy Gets Homesick in Italy
150: Lucy's Italian Movie
151: Lucy's Bicycle Trip
152: Lucy Goes to Monte Carlo
153: Return Home from Europe

Season Six (1956–1957)

154: Lucy and Bob Hope
155: Lucy Meets Orson Welles
156: Little Ricky Gets Stage Fright
157: Little Ricky Learns to Play the Drums
158: Visitor from Italy
159: Off to Florida
160: Deep Sea Fishing
161: Desert Island
162: The Ricardos Visit Cuba
163: Little Ricky's School Pageant
Special: The *I Love Lucy* Christmas Special
164: Lucy and the Loving Cup
165: Little Ricky Gets a Dog
166: Lucy and Superman
167: Lucy Wants to Move to the Country
168: Lucy Hates to Leave
169: Lucy Misses the Mertzes
170: Lucy Gets Chummy with the Neighbors
171: Lucy Raises Chickens
172: Lucy Does the Tango
173: Ragtime Band
174: Lucy's Night in Town
175: Housewarming
176: Building a Barbecue
177: Country Club Dance
178: Lucy Raises Tulips
179: The Ricardos Dedicate a Statue

The Lucille Ball-Desi Arnaz Show (1957–1960)

1: Lucy Takes a Cruise to Havana
2: The Celebrity Next Door
3: Lucy Hunts Uranium
4: Lucy Wins a Racehorse
5: Lucy Goes to Sun Valley
6: Lucy Goes to Mexico
7: Lucy Makes Room for Danny
8: Lucy Goes to Alaska
9: Lucy Wants a Career
10: Lucy's Summer Vacation
11: Milton Berle Hides Out at the Ricardos'
12: The Ricardos Go to Japan
13: Lucy Meets the Mustache

LUCY AND DESI, 1941

M Pub-1695

Love and Marriage

For all its emphasis on Lucy's wild antics, *I Love Lucy* was at heart a domestic comedy. In the very first episode that was aired ("The Girls Want to Go to a Nightclub"), the discussion centers around wedding anniversaries and celebrations. Unfortunately, divorce is also mentioned, but that was due to Lucy trying to get her own way, or rather Ethel's way. Lucy and Ethel were very much homemakers, Ricky had an outside job, and Fred was the apartment building's manager. Lucy and Ethel cooked and cleaned, vacuumed and dusted, washed laundry and dishes, and served up a lot of food and drink along the way. What made it interesting was the trouble everyone got into

LUCY AND RICKY GOT A HINT OF WHAT IT WOULD BE LIKE TO GROW OLD TOGETHER IN "THE YOUNG FANS."

while they were performing their daily duties and tasks.

As with any good domestic comedy, love and family are at the center of the show. Both couples had long, successful and happy (well, relatively happy in the case of Ethel and Fred!) marriages. The Ricardo marriage is somewhat easy to trace. When the show began in 1951, they had been married for ten years (first mention, "The Pioneers"). It's not clear how they met, although in "The Marriage License," Ricky does make mention of the fact that he might have been tricked into marriage because he didn't speak English very well, and in "The Girls Want to Go to a Nightclub," he mentions that Lucy told him that burning his address book was part of the American marriage ceremony. Also, in the later hour-long episodes, the Ricardos tell Hedda Hopper they met in Cuba while Lucy was on a cruise and Ricky was driving a cab. All hints point to a short and passionate courtship, much like the real one between Lucy and Desi.

In "The Marriage License," we learn that Ricky proposed in a lovely park in Greenwich, Connecticut, on a bench between two trees during a picnic lunch. He was so nervous he had forgotten his wallet and Lucy had to pay for the license. The couple was married by a justice of the peace at the Byram River Beagle Club (this is true of their actual marriage). We also find out that the marriage license was written incorrectly and that his last name was spelled Bicardi! All this (plus Fred's interference at the license bureau) leads Lucy to conclude that they are not legally married, so she makes Ricky do the whole thing over again, which of course leads to more hijinks and hilarity.

When Lucy discovers she is pregnant, it is a banner day for the Ricardos. She informs Ethel she's been married for eleven years, so she has no reason to believe she would be pregnant after all that time. When she returns from the doctor, however, she is on Cloud Nine, thrilled that she and Ricky will at last be parents! Ethel and Fred are equally

LUCY, DESI, AND THEIR TWO CHILDREN,
DESI JR, AND LUCIE, 1953

excited that they will be godparents (Ethel is anxious to know whether she will be a godmother or a godfather—apparently it depends on the gender of the baby!) Lucy tries to tell her husband about their wonderful news all day long, but they keep getting interrupted. Finally, in desperation, she goes to the Tropicana and hands the maitre d' a note to give to Ricky—someone in the audience is about to have "a blessed event" and would he sing a song for the happy couple? He goes around the room, singing and trying to find the couple. When he sees Lucy sitting alone, he smiles at her and moves on. Suddenly, in a moment of clarity, Ricky realizes the father-to-be is none other than he! The happy couple embraces and dances together as Ricky serenades his expectant wife.

The writers gave a total of seven episodes to the pregnancy—from announcement to birth. As soon as Lucy discovers her condition she quickly chooses names, learns how to diaper and bathe the baby, makes her "swan song" performance at Ricky's club, gets the whole gang involved in proper English lessons, arranges a baby shower for Ricky,

becomes a sculptress (so the baby won't think she has no artistic talent), and finally gives birth. The night of the birth of Ricky Ricardo, Jr. (January 19, 1953) coincided with the birth of the couple's real son and second child, Desiderio Alberto Arnaz, IV (Desi, Jr.) that morning. The scene in which Lucy is taken to the hospital is a classic one, with everyone having a job to do, but no one being able to complete his or her task. They even leave the apartment without Lucy! Finally, though, the miracle takes place and Lucy and Ricky are blessed with their one and only child. Ricky and the scenarios that go along with infants (crying, exhaustion, babysitters, lack of space, etc.) were immediately added to the scripts, adding many new storylines for the writers.

The Mertz marriage is a bit more of a mystery. In the very first aired episode, "The Girls Want to Go to a Nightclub," Ethel and Fred are about to celebrate their eighteenth wedding anniversary. About forty episodes later, in the beginning of the second season, we learn they've been married twenty-two years in the "Vacation from Marriage"

OPERATION
MERCY
CITY OF HOPE
ALL STAR   THON

Sponsored by the Greater Los Angeles Press Club

FIGHT
CANCER · LEUKEMIA · TUBERCULOSIS

5

Sat. Oct. 17 · 11 p.m. to Sun. Oct. 18 · 4 p.m.
Carthay Circle Theater

episode. And just one episode later, Lucy and Ricky surprise them on their twenty-fifth anniversary with the gift of a new TV set (that Ricky proceeds to break).

We don't know anything about the Mertz courtship or wedding, but we do know they always seem to have worked together. They were a vaudeville team in the early days of their marriage, and for the first few seasons of the show they are building owners and landlords together (although Fred seems to do most of the work, and rarely trusts Ethel with the job of collecting the rent money). Later, when they move to Connecticut to be closer to the Ricardos, they share chicken farming and egg collecting duties. While the Mertz marriage may not be the most torrid romance ever recorded, they do have a good working relationship and they do stick up for each other against Lucy and Ricky when things get heated between the two couples. They are the perfect example of an older couple who has been together for many years. The passion might be gone, but in the end there is trust, forgiveness, and an ability to work as a team that makes their marriage successful, if not perfect.

Loveable Quotes

Ricky (proposing to Lucy): Lucy, I love you madly. Lucy, I can't live without you. I know I don't deserve a wonderful girl like you. Lucy, will you marry me?

. . . . ✳ ✳ . . . .

Lucy: Husbands make me so mad. They're always promising you that they'll do something for you and then they don't do it.

Ethel: Well, that's one problem I never have with Fred.

Lucy: You don't?

Ethel: Nope, he never promises to do anything for me in the first place.

. . . . ✳ ✳ . . . .

Lucy: I love you.

Ricky: What do you want?

THE LOVE VISIBLE ON *I LOVE LUCY* WAS BASED ON THE REAL-LIFE LOVE BETWEEN LUCY AND DESI.

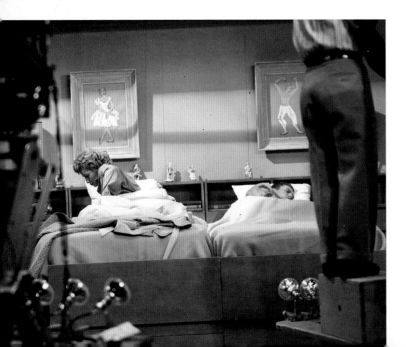

Ricky: Listen, do you know anything about rice?

Fred: Well, I had it thrown at me on one of the darkest days of my life.

Ricky: After all, if this guy is fortunate enough to still be single . . .

Lucy: What?

Ricky: I didn't mean it that way. I mean, if he's smart enough to still be single . . .

Lucy: How's that?

Ricky: There must be some word that describes what I'm trying to say.

Lucy: The word is stupid.

Ricky: All right, stupid. If the guy's stupid enough to still be single, leave him alone.

Lucy: That's better.

Lucy: Now what would you do if the first time I met you I insulted you, spilled stuff all over you, and acted like a first-class nincompoop?

Ricky: Just what I did—wait for my suit to come back from the cleaners, then marry you!

Ricky: When we got married, you said you would never take your ring off.

Lucy: When we got married, you said that dishwater would never touch these lily-white hands.

Lucy: Is Ethel there?

Fred: No.

Lucy: Well, where is she?

Fred: How should I know?

Fred and Ethel—veteran vaudevillians

For better or worse, Fred and Ethel were joined at the hip in "Lucy Goes to Scotland."

Lucy loves marriage so much she's a hopeless matchmaker, which causes her plenty of trouble in "Lucy Plays Cupid."

"Sentimental Anniversary"

Lucy: Well, she's your wife.

Fred: Did you wake me up just to rub it in?

· · · · · · · · · · · · · · · ✳ · · · · · · · · · · · · · · ·

Fred: Eventually every married woman gets the feeling that her husband wants to kill her. And she's usually right.

· · · · · · · · · · · · · · · ✳ · · · · · · · · · · · · · · ·

Ricky: Look, Lucy, this whole thing is my fault.

Lucy: *Your* fault?

Ricky: It was something that I said that started this whole thing.

Lucy: What did you say?

Ricky: "I do."

· · · · · · · · · · · · · · · ✳ · · · · · · · · · · · · · · ·

Ricky: Listen Fred, I got an awful problem on my hands.

Fred: You should have thought of that before you married her.

· · · · · · · · · · · · · · · ✳ · · · · · · · · · · · · · · ·

Lucy: Oh, I'll hang that up for you, dear.

Ricky: I can do it, honey.

Lucy: No, no, no, honey. That's what wives are for.

Fred: Oh, so that's what they're for!

· · · · · · · · · · · · · · · ✳ · · · · · · · · · · · · · · ·

THE RICARDO CHILD, LITTLE RICKY
(PLAYED BY KEITH THIBODEAUX)

Lucy: Ricky is going to give me something. Something every woman has always wanted from her husband.

Ethel: A divorce?

· · · · · · · · · · · · · · · ✳ · · · · · · · · · · · · · · ·

Lucy: Now, honey, remember when we were married, you wanted to be joined together in matrimony.

Ricky: And as I recall, it was "'til death do us part."

Lucy: Yes, that's right.

Ricky: Well, that event is about to take place right now!

· · · · · · · · · · · · · · · ✳ · · · · · · · · · · · · · · ·

Ethel: Your life should be just one gay round of nightclubs.

Lucy: Yeah, that's what I thought when I married a bandleader, but ever since we said "I do" there are so many things we don't.

Only the best of friends could pull off matching burlap.

Eternal BFFs

Equally important as the theme of love and marriage on *I Love Lucy* is the theme of friendship. How could Lucy have pulled off even half her wild stunts had she not had best gal pal Ethel by her side? And how many times did Ricky turn to Fred for advice or help when he needed to cheat on a bet or teach Lucy a lesson? Countless. It's not even possible to imagine the *I Love Lucy* show without the Mertzes, although that was actually the way the pilot episode was written.

At the heart of the friendship theme is the comradeship between Lucy and Ethel. As Lucille Ball and Vivian Vance were in real life, Lucy Ricardo and Ethel Mertz were sisters of the heart. They fought and debated, they were at times jealous and competitive, but at the end of the day they would have done anything for each other. They were side by side at Kramer's Kandy Kitchen; they dressed as Martians and climbed the Empire State Building; they performed together on stage numerous times; they somehow hid seven hundred pounds of beef in the basement; they wore burlap sacks and horse-feed bags on the streets of Paris; they were club co-presidents; they went to charm school and they went to jail. And when she found out she was pregnant, who was the first person Lucy told? It was Ethel, of course! It's impossible to even imagine Lucy Ricardo without Ethel Mertz, and because of that, this dynamic duo set the bar for future female friendships on TV. Consider Laverne and Shirley, Kate and Allie, Mary and Rhoda, Wilma and Betty, and Cagney and Lacey—where would they have been without Lucy and Ethel?

Most of the time, Lucy and Ethel were on the same side. Often the plots would pit the women against the men. Sometimes it was a bet, like the time they all went back to the year 1900, or when they switched jobs with their hubbies, or hid a huge tuna in their hotel room. The scheme was usually Lucy's idea—such as going on television to win a trip to Hawaii or make a $1 million selling salad dressing. Sometimes they were trying to save a situation—such as when they had to rebuild a barbecue at midnight

or fill the hen house with five dozen eggs. Although the plans were rarely her idea, Ethel invariably went along with them. What would have been the fun had she said no? Lucy would have had no one to turn to. Carolyn Appleby was certainly not going to help Lucy sneak into the Tropicana dressed as a bass fiddle, was she?

Sometimes their friendship was tested, and that was usually when they wanted the same thing. Once they both wanted to be club president, and who can forget the time they bought identical dresses and neither wanted to give hers up? Sometimes they coveted the same role in a play. In those cases either Lucy won because Ricky was the host of the show, or Ethel won because she was the one with talent. Once they even fought because Fred asked Lucy to buy Ethel's birthday present for him; Lucy chose something she thought Ethel would love and Ethel couldn't imagine why Lucy thought she would have given those hostess pants a second look. Still other times it was Ricar-

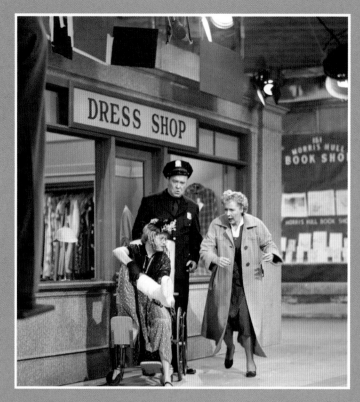

LUCY AND ETHEL NEVER LEARN THAT IT'S NOT A GOOD IDEA TO GO INTO BUSINESS TOGETHER.

THE GENUINE FRIENDSHIP BETWEEN THE STARS IS VISIBLE IN THIS SHOT BETWEEN TAKES OF "LUCY AND ETHEL BUY THE SAME DRESS."

do versus Mertz and all the parties were involved. Remember the time Lucy and Ricky tried to break their lease by holding an impromptu dance party on the ceiling above the Mertz apartment? Whatever the problem is though, we can always count on the friendship surviving. By the end of the episode, everyone has made up and things are back to normal.

The same is true for the men. Although they did not lean on each other in the same way their wives did, there were a lot of times Ricky and Fred needed to rely on each other. Often it was to hide something from their wives—such as the time Ricky did not want Lucy to know where the Vitameatavegamin commercial was being filmed. Or the

time the Ricardos were fighting, and Ricky used Fred to help him make Lucy believe the apartment was on fire.

Other times they teamed up to beat their wives at their own game—such as when they honored their wives' wishes for equal rights by refusing to pay for their meals, therefore earning Lucy and Ethel jobs washing dishes in the restaurant kitchen. In Paris they had a tailor whip up dresses and hats from burlap bags, and allowed their wives to traipse around the streets looking like fashion nightmares. And what about the time Ricky made the dinner (*arroz con pollo*) and Fred made the dessert (chocolate layer cake)—now *that* was teamwork!

Sometimes Fred really messed up. After all, he's the one who told Ricky to tell Lucy their marriage license was invalid. And how about the time he sent "forgive me" flowers to Lucy from Ricky, and signed his own name! Oftentimes the fellas messed up together, like the time they made a bet about gossiping, and then had simultaneous "dreams" about a juicy piece of gossip concerning the neighbors. Later they pretend to "catch" their wives gossiping by listening through the furnace pipe!

When it wasn't gals vs. guys, or Ricardos vs. Mertzes, it could be Lucy, Ethel, and Fred against Ricky, such as the time Ricky needs a western act for his nightclub but doesn't want to pay the trio. More often it was Ricky, Ethel, and Fred against Lucy. Remember the time Lucy snuck into their barbershop quartet? Or how about the time Lucy wrote a novel about them all, but they didn't like how they were portrayed, so they burned it in the fireplace. Talk about ganging up on a girl!

There were, of course, other friendships and acquaintances on the show. Lucy and Ethel had their club friends such as Carolyn Appleby, Grace Munson, and Marion Strong, although sometimes "frenemies" would be a better way to describe these ladies. Do you remember Lucy "dropping in" on an unprepared Carolyn at home, or the same two ladies fighting over whose son's birthday party should be on Saturday? It was no different when the families moved to Connecticut—Ethel couldn't stand her new Connecticut neighbor Betty Ramsey until they realized they had grown up together, after which they were joined at the hip.

Ricky had own pals, like Marco (played by Marco Rizo, Desi's real-life musical director) and the other boys in the band, as well as his Spanish-speaking amigos from Cuba. Later in the series, he rubbed elbows and made friends with famous

LUCY AND ETHEL COULD ALWAYS COUNT ON EACH OTHER.

Lucy, Ethel, and country neighbor Betty Ramsey

Hollywood celebrities like William Holden, John Wayne, Richard Widmark, and Cornel Wilde. Fred had other friendships too—some lodge buddies, as well as life-long vaudeville pals such as Ted Kurtz.

However, while these adjunct relationships were often important for the strength of storylines, the heart of the matter was that the Ricardos and the Mertzes were, and are, forever linked. They are forever associated in our cultural memory. They love each other, and their fans around the world love them—as couples, as a trio, and as a quartet—in whatever formation the writers placed them. They are the basis of everything we love about *I Love Lucy*; they teach us about life, loyalty, jealousy, teamwork, trust, and love. What better lessons could the world learn?

The writers often worked in the names of personal friends and Desilu employees, as well as places important to the cast, into the scripts. Throughout the series one hears mentions of:

THE STARS AT THE 1954 EMMY AWARDS

Harry Ackerman, CBS producer

Albaquerque, New Mexico, Vivian's childhood home

Lillian Appleby, Lucy's childhood teacher

Bill Asher, *I Love Lucy* director

"Bob and Madelyn," Bob Carroll, Jr. and Madelyn Pugh, *I Love Lucy* writers

Celoron, New York, Lucy's hometown

Chautauqua Lake, near Lucy's childhood home

Ericksons, childhood neighbors of Lucy

"Gregory and Joanne," children of Jess Oppenheimer

Dr. Joseph Harris, Lucille Ball's obstetrician

Havana, Cuba, Desi's hometown

LUCY AND DESI SURROUNDED BY FRIENDS AND FAMILY AT A COSTUME PARTY AT THE DESILU RANCH IN CHATSWORTH.

Lucy and writer Bob Carroll, Jr. compare whiskers.

Andrew Hickox, Arnaz family business manager

Hunt, Lucy's mother's family name

Jamestown, New York, Lucy's birthplace

Dan Jenkins, *TV Guide* writer

"Philip and Morris," *I Love Lucy*'s sponsor was Philip Morris

Charlie Pomerantz, Desilu employee

Dr. (Marcus) Rabwin, Arnaz family friend/physician

Santiago de Cuba, Desi's birthplace and childhood home

Vivian Vance and writer Bob Carroll, Jr.

Flo Pauline Lopus, childhood friend of Lucy

Cleo Morgan, Lucy's cousin

Argyle Nelson, *I Love Lucy* production manager

Peterson, family name of Lucy's stepfather

"Scott and Pamela," Lucy's niece and nephew

Marion Strong Van Vlack, childhood friend of Lucy

Norman Van Vlack, husband of Marion

Desi and Lucille, a happy couple ready for dinner, 1941. They were still newlyweds then.

Lucy the Foodie

One would expect a lot of cooking and eating to be going on in a domestic comedy, and *I Love Lucy* certainly does not disappoint. In almost every episode there is food being prepared, bought, eaten, or cleaned up. Coffee is readily available at all hours of the day and offered to whomever walks through the door. Dinner parties, club luncheons, and fancy breakfasts are often planned and consumed. Sometimes bets are placed with the prize being breakfast in bed or a restaurant dinner for the winners. There is just no getting away from it. Food is a large part of the *I Love Lucy* show.

Although some women, particularly those who worked outside the home during the war effort, were becoming less and less interested in being housewives, many more were still happy to stay home and be "domestic engineers." Most TV wives of the 1950s were of the old-fashioned variety. Harriet Nelson (*Ozzie and Harriet*), Margaret Anderson (*Father Knows Best*), June Cleaver (*Leave it to Beaver*), and Donna Stone (*The Donna Reed Show*) were all white, middle class, and suburban. They were also typical pie-baking, sandwich-serving moms. Lucy Ricardo was much the same way. She did not dream of being freed from the burden of the kitchen. Lucy generally cooked from scratch, whether it was chicken or pancakes. She enjoyed cooking for Ricky and hosting club luncheons and dinner parties. She loved making surprise treats for Little Ricky when he came home from school. In that way, and perhaps only in that way, she was very much "average."

One thing that was changing for the average American family was the actual food they were eating. During World War II, food businesses went into production making meals for soldiers and sailors. The maxim, "an army marches on its stomach," is indeed true. Food had to be easy to make, portable, and often freezable or powdered. On the home front, since all metals were rationed during the war, frozen food actually cost a housewife fewer ration points than its canned counterpart.

After the war ended in 1945 and our "boys" came home from Europe and Asia, the businesses that had been producing these military meals had to find another avenue

LUCY LIKED TO COOK, BUT THE KITCHEN IN THE ARNAZ HOME WAS MASTERED BY DESI.

A CATCHER'S MITT AT THE RICARDO BREAKFAST
TABLE CAME IN HANDY TO CATCH TOAST SENT
AIRBORNE BY THE TOASTER.

to sell their products. The problem was that they were producing wartime food for a peacetime market place. Food had been designed and produced for soldiers in the tropical jungles of the Philippines, and the frozen forests of Bavaria. Companies had learned how to can foods (soups, Spam), dehydrate them (milk, coffee, lemonade, orange juice), and freeze them (vegetables, French fries). The problem became how to make these foods appetizing enough for the post-war housewife to continue to use them. What is good during time of war rationing, or in a naval submarine, is not necessarily good when there are other options.

Ease of preparation was certainly a good marketing tool. General Mills came out with a product called "Pyequick," which was a piecrust along with a bag of dehydrated apples all in one box. No longer would Mrs. America have to make dough from scratch, shape it, cut apples, and add spices.

All that could be accomplished in about five minutes, leaving her time to spend with her children, or cleaning her new suburban home. Frozen, refrigerated, and pre-baked piecrusts still exist today, although the novelty of the "pie in a box" did not take off with the American public.

Another product developed in the early 1950s to make life easier for mom was produced by the Swanson frozen foods company; they called it the "TV dinner." Television was still a new medium, but by the middle of the decade, about 60 percent of American households owned one. Making a frozen, pre-cooked meal and connecting it to the television by virtue of its name was the perfect way to get housewives interested. Just heat it up and serve casually in front of the TV. The trays used for these dinners looked like those the soldiers used in the mess halls—a rectangle broken up into sections, one large for the meat, and smaller ones for the starch, a vegetable, and possibly a dessert treat. All of a sudden, tired moms could turn on the oven, pop in a frozen dinner or two, and half an hour later—*voilà*—dinner is served.

Not only would housewives be saved from the tasks of setting the table and cooking the meal, but cleanup would be a breeze. With more and more "menu" choices, it soon worked out that each person could have his choice of meal—Billy could have turkey, while Susie chose meatloaf. Of course, no red-blooded American woman would serve such a thing to her mother-in-law or her husband's boss, but for the kids on a night when she had other pressing matters, these meals would definitely do in a pinch.

Also new on the market were drinks and dessert in powered form—Jell-O, pudding, and Cool Whip had made their way to the shelves of American markets and were being consumed by thousands of children. Kool-Aid was becoming popular, and powdered lemonade was also being discovered by housewives tired of squeezing lemons for their children's roadside stands. Frozen popsicles were a hit with kids, and the ice cream man and his musical truck were soon making their way through suburban and city streets across the country.

On *I Love Lucy*, all this food consumption was apparent,

although Lucy didn't seem to take part in the frozen food revolution. We never saw her take a bag of broccoli out of the freezer, or whip up a glass of Tang. Instead, Lucy was seen squeezing fresh oranges for Ricky's juice, or baking a cake from scratch for the PTA meeting. It would be a decade or more before this new way of cooking and eating would take over American TV. In the 1970s, Mary Tyler Moore's character, Mary Richards, would be seen heating up TV dinners, or ordering delivery pizza. As for our Lucy, she is forever enshrined in the "TV Mom" Hall of Fame.

Some of the foods on *I Love Lucy* actually became important to the plot of the episode. Sometimes the food was actually like another character. Who could forget all those chocolates Lucy and Ethel ate, or the escargot Lucy was served at the Parisian café? Or how about the yards-long loaf of bread she baked in her kitchen, or the pizza she desperately tried to toss at the pizzeria? Who could forget the time when Ricky and Fred made chicken and rice for dinner—and it ended up on the ceiling and the floor? And of course, Lucy was famous for catching the toast as it flew out of the toaster! Considering the extent that food and drink played a valuable and noteworthy role in the series, following is a guide to the food and drink eaten, discussed, or mentioned in each episode.

Recipes included

Lucy got more than she bargained for when she made bread in "Pioneer Women."

****Featured recipes

Pilot episode: toast, pie, coffee

"Lucy Thinks Ricky is Trying to Murder Her": cheese, crackers, coffee

"The Girls Want to Go to a Nightclub": steak, gravy, raw onions, beer, champagne

"Be a Pal": egg, coffee cake, grapefruit, toast, jam, donuts, frijoles, tacos, enchiladas, guacamole, tamales, huevos rancheros, coffee

"The Diet": oysters, celery, steak, potatoes, biscuits, green beans, bread, coffee

"The Quiz Show": pears, coffee

"The Audition": pie

"The Séance": grapefruit, eggs, toast, coffee

"Men Are Messy": banana, walnuts, oranges, chicken, beer

"Drafted": cookies, tea, milk, coffee

"The Fur Coat": coffee

"Lucy is Jealous of Girl Singer": *arroz con pollo* **

"The Adagio": cake, coffee

"The Benefit": chicken

"The Amateur Hour": cookies, coffee, milk

"Lucy Plays Cupid": toast, steak, lima beans, gum drops, biscuits, soup, coffee, orange juice, tomato juice, Elderberry wine

"Lucy Fakes Illness": cookies, coffee

"Lucy Writes a Play": sandwich

"Breaking the Lease": drinks

"The Ballet": pie

"The Young Fans": toast, coffee

"New Neighbors": turkey leg, soft-boiled eggs, coffee

"Fred and Ethel Fight": roast beef, gravy, peanut butter sandwich, mashed potatoes, string beans, grape juice, soda

"The Moustache": buttered popcorn

"The Gossip": eggs, ham, toast, honey dew melon, jam, strawberries, coffee, orange juice, hot chocolate, Eggs Benedict **

"Pioneer Women": homemade bread, coffee, homemade butter **

"The Marriage License": rice (thrown), picnic lunch, chicken salad sandwich, peanut butter sandwich

"The Kleptomaniac": pancakes, potatoes, coffee

"Cuban Pals": cookies, hors d'oevres, coffee, wine

"The Freezer": eggs, grapefruit, soup, seven hundred pounds of beef, coffee

"The Publicity Agent": coffee

"Lucy Gets Ricky on the Radio": popcorn, sandwiches, lemonade

"Lucy's Schedule": waxed fruit, mints, salad, stuffed pork chops, steak, peas, eggs, split pea soup, sweet rolls, biscuits, cheese baked potatoes, asparagus, Hollandaise sauce, coffee

"Ricky Thinks He's Getting Bald": grapefruit, toast, jam, nuts, pretzels, coffee

"Ricky Asks for a Raise": cheesecake, coffee

"The Anniversary Present": rice, scrambled eggs, coffee, juice

"The Operetta": cookies, coffee

"Job Switching": eggs, toast, chicken, rice, hash browns, chocolates, chocolate cake, coffee, orange juice

"Vacation from Marriage": coffee, beer

"The Courtroom": cake

"Redecorating": sandwich, double chocolate malted

"Ricky Loses His Voice": toast, bacon, poached eggs, orange juice

"Sales Resistance": potato

"The Inferiority Complex": candy, steak, pork chops, roast beef, eggs, toast, coffee, orange juice

"The Club Election": pork and beans, iced tea, beer

"The Black Eye": steak, cookies, ice cream, banana

"Lucy Changes Her Mind": roast beef, lamb chops, sirloin steak, ravioli foo young, sandwich, pork chops, shrimp cocktail, chicken chow pizza, coffee, milk

"Lucy is Enceinte": sandwich, celery, coffee, milk

"Pregnant Women Are Unpredictable": waffles, champagne

"Lucy Hires an English Tutor": dill pickles, papaya juice milkshake

Behind the scenes—Lucy's Lazy Susan was a convenience at mealtime.

"Ricky Has Labor Pains": roast beef, steak, potatoes, sardines, hot fudge, pistachio ice cream, fried egg sandwich, beer

"Lucy Goes to the Hospital": cookies, milk

"No Children Allowed": sandwiches, tea

"Lucy Hires a Maid": peanut butter sandwich, jelly, roast beef, lettuce, toast, coffee, orange juice

"Lucy's Last Birthday": cake, coffee

"The Ricardos Change Apartments": cake, roast, meatloaf, sandwich, apple pie, ice cream sodas

"Lucy Wants New Furniture": bread, butter, steak, green beans, potatoes, eggs, sausage, toast, coffee, orange juice

"The Camping Trip": trout

"Ricky and Fred Are TV Fans": potato chips, pretzels, fudge, ginger ale

"Never Do Business with Friends": cold cuts, bread

"Ricky's LIFE Story": baby food, banana, *arroz con pollo***

"The Girls Go Into Business": soda

"Lucy and Ethel Buy the Same Dress": club meeting refreshments, punch

"Equal Rights": steak, spaghetti, meatballs, pizza, green salad, coffee

Lucy and Ethel, out to eat in "The Black Wig"

"Lucy Tells the Truth": coffee

"Redecorating the Mertzes' Apartment": salami sandwich, beer

"Too Many Crooks": peanuts, lemonade

"Lucy Has Her Eyes Examined": roast, peas, vanilla ice cream

"Ricky's Old Girlfriend": cake, hors d'oeuvres, coffee

"The Million-Dollar Idea": salad, meatloaf, potatoes, pastries, salad dressing (oil, onions, salt)

"Ricky Minds the Baby": brownies, frijoles, tortillas, oatmeal, coffee, wine, Spanish omelet **

"The Charm School": cake, coffee

"Sentimental Anniversary": cake, roast, potatoes, champagne

"Fan Magazine Interview": eggs, bacon, crepes Suzette, steak, shrimp cocktail, eggs Benedict, waffles, sausage, ham, coffee, orange juice, half-and-half

"Oil Wells": eggs, bacon, coffee, orange juice

"Ricky Loses His Temper": walnuts, crackers, cottage cheese, tomato juice

"Home Movies": candy, coffee

"Bonus Bucks": oatmeal

"Ricky's Hawaiian Vacation": honey, pie, eggs, coffee

"Lucy is Envious": meat, potatoes, celery

"The Black Wig": coffee

"The Diner": blintzes, toast, scrambled eggs, hamburgers, tortillas, mashed bananas, pancakes, hotdogs, hash, pie, coffee, cream, orange juice

"Tennessee Ernie Hangs On": bread, roast, flour, canned goods, milk

"The Sublease": hot fudge sundae

"The Business Manager": waffles, cereal, melon, whole wheat bread, round steak, oranges, green beans, crackers, flour, chocolate cookies, Devil's Food cake, lemon pie, sugar, chicken, strawberry jam, Corn Flakes, coffee, milk, half-and-half, sherry

"Mertz and Kurtz": beef, potatoes, green beans, gravy, rolls

"Lucy Cries Wolf": toast, coffee

"The Matchmaker": chicken, bacon, eggs, toast, chocolates, coffee, orange juice

"Mr. and Mrs. TV Show": waffles, coffee

"Ricky's Movie Offer": melon

"Ricky's Screen Test": cup of sugar, coffee

"Lucy's Mother-in-Law": *arroz con pollo***

"Ethel's Birthday": cake, coffee

"Ricky's Contract": French toast, sandwich, coffee

"California, Here We Come!": picnic basket

"First Stop": pecan pralines, stale cheese sandwiches, grapes, steak sandwich, French fries, cole slaw, roast beef, fried chicken, biscuits, turkey dinner, cranberry sauce, green salad, peach shortcake, stuffing, baked potatoes

"Ethel's Hometown": candy, ice cream, soda

"L.A. at Last!": Derby tossed salad, spaghetti and meatballs, meat sauce, veal cutlet, cream pie, coffee, Cobb Salad**

"Don Juan and the Starlets": chocolates

"Lucy Gets in Pictures": hot fudge sundae, banana split, pineapple soda, chocolate malt

"The Hedda Hopper Story": cake, coffee, tea

"Don Juan is Shelved": coffee

"Hollywood Anniversary": grapefruit, pancakes, coffee, champagne

"The Star Upstairs": rolls, cold cuts, cheese, coffee

"In Palm Springs": chocolates, cake, coffee, lemonade

"Harpo Marx": chocolates, cake, coffee

"The Tour": grapefruit

"Lucy Visits Grauman's": caviar, cake, hors d'oeuvres, punch

"Lucy and John Wayne": toast, eggs, coffee

"Homecoming": roast pig, cake, eggs, bacon, toast, coffee, orange juice

"The Ricardos are Interviewed": candy

"Nursery School": cake

"Bon Voyage": fruit baskets, champagne

"Second Honeymoon": coffee, soda

"The Fox Hunt": tea

"Lucy Goes to Scotland": McGillicuddy Foo Young, McGillicuddy Burger

"Paris at Last": wine, *escargots à la Bourguignonne*****

"Lucy Meets Charles Boyer": pastries, oranges, coffee

"Lucy Gets a Paris Gown": bread, butter, steak, French fries, broccoli with Hollandaise sauce, shrimp salad, pastries, bologna, cheese, lettuce, mustard, roast chicken, coffee, milk

"Lucy in the Swiss Alps": cheese sandwiches

"Lucy Gets Homesick in Italy": chocolates, birthday cake, gelato

"Lucy's Italian Movie": grapes, wine

"Lucy's Bicycle Trip": bread, cheese, milk

"Return Home from Europe": Italian cheese, steak, apricot pie

"Lucy and Bob Hope": popcorn, hotdogs ("red hots!"), mustard, relish

"Lucy Meets Orson Welles": apple, coffee

"Little Ricky Learns to Play the Drums": toast, oatmeal, eggs, roast chicken, coffee, milk, orange juice

"Little Ricky Gets Stage Fright": sandwich, coffee

"Visitor from Italy": cake, pizza, coffee

"Off to Florida": watercress sandwiches, coffee

"Deep-Sea Fishing": tuna

"Desert Island": coconuts, lemonade

"The Ricardos Visit Cuba": coffee

"Little Ricky's School Pageant": peanut butter sandwich, coffee, milk

"Lucy Wants to Move to the Country": homemade butter, homemade grape jelly, eggs, coffee, tomato juice

"Lucy Hates to Leave": hot mustard, bread, deli meats, cheese, coffee, milk, chicken fricassee****

"Lucy Misses the Mertzes": fruit basket

"Lucy Gets Chummy with the Neighbors": toast, jelly, coffee

"Lucy Raises Chickens": cake, sandwiches, chicken, coffee, lemonade

"Lucy Does the Tango": eggs, toast, coffee

"Ragtime Band": fried bananas, *arroz con pollo*****

"Lucy's Night in Town": cereal, eggs, toast, roast beef, lima beans, mashed potatoes, steak, seafood, rolls, butter, broiled chicken, coffee, juice, orangeade

"Housewarming": cake, Jell-O, sandwiches, tuna salad, coffee

"Building a Barbecue": hamburgers, macaroni and cheese, coffee

"Country Club Dance": toast, rolls, potato salad, olives, beef, coffee

"Lucy Raises Tulips": lemonade

"The Ricardos Dedicate a Statue": cold cuts, bread, peanut butter and jelly sandwiches

Advertising popular food brands of the 1950s:

IN THE KITCHEN WITH DESI (AND LITTLE LUCIE ON RIGHT). DESI WAS KNOWN TO BE A WONDERFUL COOK.

Selected Recipes

Arroz con Pollo

This dish turned up regularly on the Ricardos' dinner table, as it was Ricky's favorite.

Yield: 6 servings

Ingredients

Salt, pepper, and cumin

Olive oil

8 chicken thighs, bone in, skin on

1 large onion, chopped

1 large green pepper, chopped

1 large red pepper, chopped

4 cloves garlic, mashed

12 oz. bottle of beer

3½ cups chicken broth

8 oz. can of tomato sauce

1 bay leaf

2 teaspoons oregano

2 teaspoons ground cumin

1½ teaspoons salt

½ teaspoon black pepper

3½ cups yellow rice*

½ cup frozen baby green peas

Season the chicken lightly with salt, pepper, and a little cumin. Place olive oil in frying pan and turn heat to medium. Place chicken in pan when hot. Remove the chicken when it is browned on both sides.

Add a little more olive oil to the same pan you fried the chicken in, and sauté the onion and chopped peppers until browned. Add the mashed garlic and cook an additional minute or two, stirring frequently.

Pour the beer and chicken broth into a large covered pot. Add the browned chicken pieces, cooked onions and peppers, tomato sauce, bay leaf, oregano, cumin, salt, and pepper. Bring to a rolling boil. Reduce heat, cover, and cook on low for 15 minutes.

Add the uncooked rice. Bring to a boil and reduce heat. When the rice has absorbed most of the liquid, cover and simmer on low for 30 to 45 minutes, or until the rice is fully cooked.

Add the frozen peas during the last five minutes of cooking.

***Note:** If you have trouble finding yellow rice, you can buy white and add a packet of Sazon seasoning, for flavor and color.

Eggs Benedict

Lucy once served this up to impress a reporter who was interviewing Ricky for a fan magazine.

Yield: 4 servings

Ingredients

4 egg yolks

3½ tablespoons lemon juice

Pinch of ground white pepper

⅛ teaspoon Worcestershire sauce

1 tablespoon water

1 cup butter, melted

¼ teaspoon salt

1 teaspoon distilled white vinegar

8 eggs

8 strips Canadian-style bacon

4 English muffins, split

2 tablespoon butter, softened

To make the Hollandaise sauce: Fill the bottom of a double boiler part-way with water. Make sure that water does not touch the top pan. Bring water to a simmer. In the top of the double boiler, whisk together egg yolks, lemon juice, white pepper, Worcestershire sauce, and water.

Add the butter to egg yolk mixture 1 or 2 tablespoons at a time while whisking yolks constantly. If Hollandaise begins to get too thick, add a teaspoon or two of hot water. Continue whisking until all butter is added. Whisk in salt, then remove from heat. To keep it warm, place a lid on the pan.

Preheat the oven to the broiler setting.*

To poach eggs: Fill a saucepan with 3 inches of water. Bring water to a simmer, then add vinegar. Carefully break eggs into simmering water, and allow them to cook for 2½ to 3 minutes. The yolks should still be soft in the center. Remove eggs from water with a slotted spoon and set on a warm plate.

While eggs are poaching, brown the bacon in a skillet over medium-high heat, and toast the English muffins on a baking sheet under the broiler, or in a toaster.

Spread toasted muffins with softened butter, and top each one with a slice of bacon, followed by one poached egg. Place one muffin on each plate and drizzle with Hollandaise sauce. Serve immediately with coffee, juice, and fruit.

*Note: When you put food in the oven and set it to broil you have to leave the oven door ajar or you end up with black food and smoke very quickly!

Swedish Rye Bread

Swedish rye bread was a favorite of Lucille Ball's. Growing up in Jamestown, Lucy lived among many first- and second-generation Swedish immigrants (including her step-grandparents, the Petersens), and their bread was one of her favorite foods. After she moved out to California, she used to have this kind of bread shipped to her from the Jones Bakery in Jamestown. Note all the kneading and rising you'll have to do—just like Lucy!

Yield: 3 loaves

Ingredients

1½ (0.6 oz.) cakes compressed fresh yeast

1½ cups warm water

1½ cups warm milk

1 tablespoon salt

¼ cup molasses

1 cup packed brown sugar

⅓ cup melted shortening

3 cups rye flour

6 cups bread flour

Dissolve yeast in warm water.

Scald milk in a hot pan. Be careful not to burn it. Transfer milk to a large bowl, and add salt, molasses, brown sugar, and melted shortening. Cool to lukewarm and add dissolved yeast. Add rye flour, beating with mixer. Gradually beat in white flour. Place dough in a greased bowl, and turn to coat the surface. Cover with a damp towel, and allow dough to rise until double in bulk in a warm place.

Punch down the dough, and place on a lightly floured board. Knead until dough becomes elastic, and does not stick to the board. Allow it to rest for 5 minutes. Divide dough into 3 equal portions, and shape into loaves. Place in greased 9"x 5" bread pans. Let rise in a warm place until double in bulk.

Bake at 375°F for 35 to 40 minutes.

Homemade Butter

Place heavy cream in a small jar (a baby food jar works well). Then, shake. You will have to shake until your hand feels like it will fall off, or you develop arms like Gorgeous George.

Spanish Omelet

This traditional Spanish dish is called tortilla de patatas. Lucy once thinks Ricky has made one for the baby, but in truth he was enjoying it himself.

Yield: 4 servings

Ingredients

Salt

5 medium baking potatoes, peeled and sliced

Olive oil

½ yellow onion, chopped

3 cloves garlic, minced

5 eggs

Salt

Lightly sprinkle the baking potatoes with salt.

Heat the olive oil in a large skillet and add the potato slices carefully, so the oil doesn't splatter. Keep the slices separated so they will not stick together. Cook, turning occasionally, over medium heat for 5 minutes. Add the onions and garlic and cook until the potatoes are tender. Drain into a colander, leaving about 3 tablespoons of oil in the skillet.

In a large bowl, whisk the eggs with a pinch of salt. Add the potatoes, and stir to coat with the egg. Add the egg-coated potatoes to the very hot oil in the skillet, spreading them evenly to completely cover the base of the skillet. Lower the heat to medium and continue to cook, shaking the pan frequently, until mixture is half set.

Invert the omelet onto a plate. Add 1 tablespoon oil to the pan and slide the omelet back into the skillet on its uncooked side. Cook until completely set. Allow the omelet to cool, and then cut it into wedges. Season with salt and pepper (optional).

Cobb Salad

This salad was invented at the Brown Derby in the 1930s, and named after owner Robert Cobb. Lovely in a large glass bowl, it is more than a salad; it is a meal in itself (unless, of course, you dump it over William Holden's head!).

Yield: 4–6 servings

Ingredients

3 hard-cooked eggs, peeled

8 bacon slices

1 head romaine lettuce, sliced into thin ribbons

2 cups chopped watercress lettuce (tough stems removed)

4 cups diced cooked turkey or chicken

2 avocados, pitted, peeled, and diced

2 tomatoes, chopped

¼ pound Roquefort or bleu cheese, crumbled

1 oz. Roquefort or bleu cheese for dressing

¼ cup red wine vinegar

1 teaspoon Worcestershire sauce

½ teaspoon Dijon mustard

1 clove garlic, minced

¼ teaspoon coarse salt

½ teaspoon coarsely ground black pepper

⅓ cup extra virgin olive oil

Cut the hard-cooked eggs into half-inch dice. Set aside.

In a large frying pan over medium heat, fry the bacon until crisp. Transfer to paper towels to drain some of the oil. When cool, crumble and set aside.

Make a bed of romaine lettuce on a platter or shallow bowl. Arrange the eggs, bacon, watercress, turkey or chicken, avocados, tomatoes, and cheese in neat rows atop the lettuce, covering the lettuce almost completely.

In a small bowl, whisk together the vinegar, Worcestershire sauce, mustard, garlic, salt, and pepper. Using a fork, mash in the remaining 1 ounce of cheese to make a paste. Slowly drizzle in the olive oil to form a thick dressing.

Pour a little of the dressing over the salad and serve immediately. Bring the remaining dressing to the table.

Escargots à la Bourguignonne

This recipe for snails in parsley butter is one Lucy Ricardo would rather forget, as would the chef she insulted by asking for ketchup.

Yield: 3 servings

Ingredients

4 oz. unsalted butter, softened

1½ garlic cloves, peeled and minced

⅛ cup minced parsley

½ small shallot, peeled and minced

1 teaspoon salt

¼ teaspoon freshly ground black pepper

¼ teaspoon freshly grated nutmeg

½ tablespoon white wine

½ teaspoon cognac

12 snail shells, cleaned

12 canned giant snails

Sea salt

In a mixing bowl, beat together butter, garlic, parsley, shallot, salt, pepper, nutmeg, wine, and cognac. Cover and refrigerate for at least 4 hours, or overnight.

Preheat oven to 400° F.

Using a butter knife, fill each snail shell with about ½ teaspoon butter mixture. Push a snail into each shell. Fill shells to the rim with remaining parsley butter. Cover the bottom of a baking pan with sea salt and arrange escargots butter side up. Bake until butter sizzles, about 10 minutes.

Chicken Fricassee

This dish was brought up when the Ricardos were staying in the Mertzes' apartment, before they moved to Connecticut and became chicken farmers. It's a safe bet they never brought it up around the chickens!

Yield: 6–8 servings

Ingredients

12 chicken thighs

2 (12 oz) packages hot sausage, sliced

5 green onions, chopped

1 white onion, chopped

1 cup vegetable oil

1 cup all-purpose flour

8 cups water

5 stalks celery, chopped

2 tablespoons Cajun seasoning

2 teaspoons cayenne pepper

2 teaspoons salt

2 teaspoons ground black pepper

1 teaspoon minced garlic

Sauté chicken and sausage in a skillet for 4 to 5 minutes. Remove meat from skillet, add green onions and white onion, and sauté until browned. Set aside.

To make the roux: In a small saucepan stir together oil and flour over low heat; cook until color is caramel and mixture is reduced to 1 cup of roux. Set aside.

Put water in a large pot. Add the chicken, sausage, onion mixture, celery, Cajun seasoning, cayenne pepper, salt, black pepper, and garlic. Bring all to a boil and cook for 20 minutes. Add ½ cup roux and stir together; the mixture should be on the thick side. If necessary, add the remaining ½ cup roux.

Reduce heat to medium low and simmer uncovered for 2 hours, stirring occasionally. Serve with rice or potatoes.

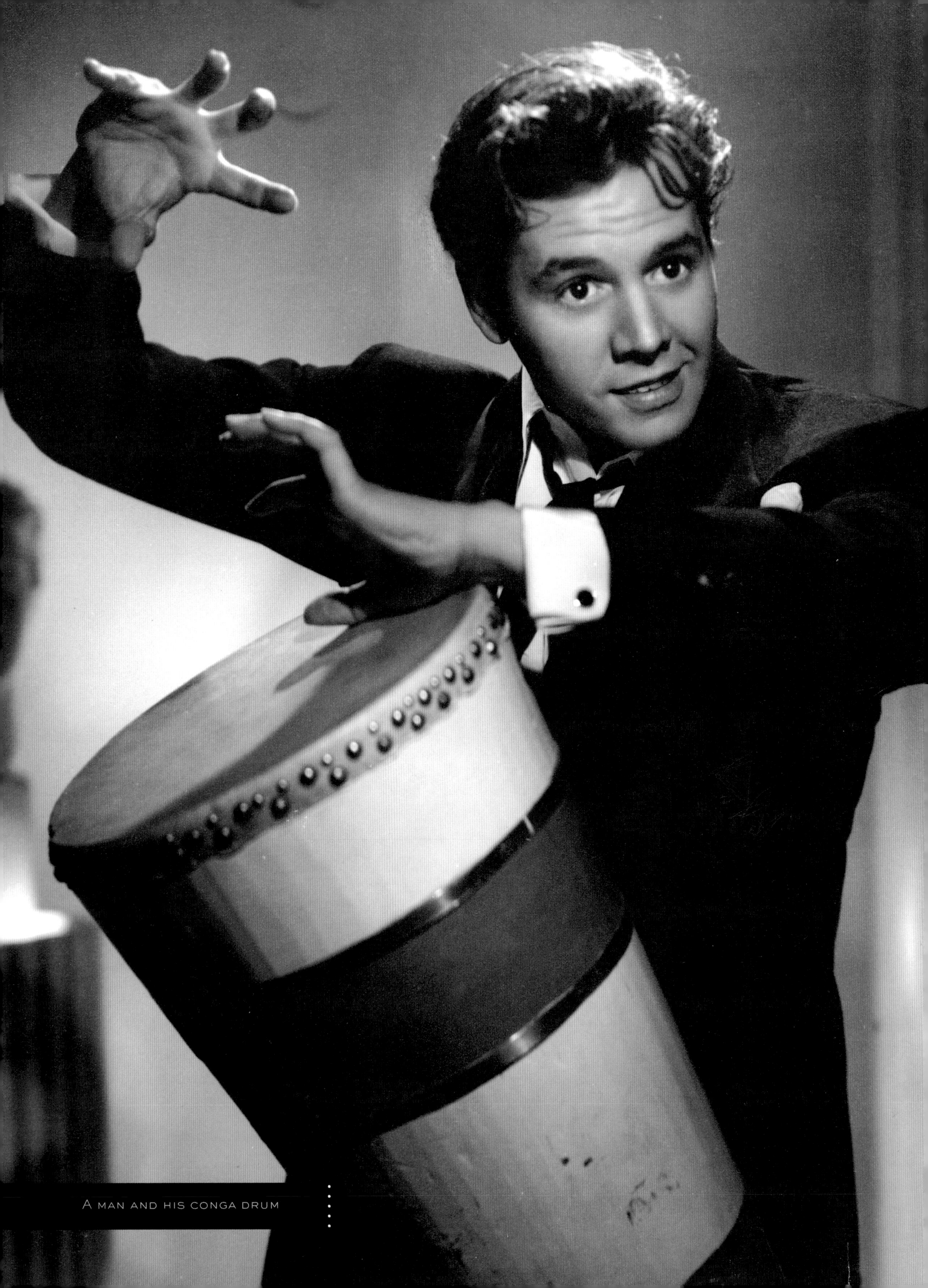

A man and his conga drum

The Latin Influence

In 2011, Latin performers, singers, and actors can be found on radio, in concert, on iPods, on television, and in movies. All Americans would recognize the names and talents of Gloria Estefan, Jennifer Lopez, George Lopez, Carlos Santana, Sofía Vergara, and Shakira. All of those entertainers owe a debt of gratitude to people like Desi Arnaz, Carmen Miranda, Xavier Cugat, and Ricardo Montalban for breaking that cultural barrier in the early part of the twentieth century. We don't think of it much, six decades after the fact, but when Desi Arnaz became Ricky Ricardo on a number-one American TV program in 1951, it was a big deal in many corners of the country.

The Arnaz marriage was considered "interracial" at the time, and CBS did not want Desi to be Lucy's husband on the show due to the potential controversy. It did not matter that Desi spoke English, was married to an American, had lived in the U.S. for almost twenty years, had graduated from high school in Florida, and was a patriotic American citizen who sold war bonds, voted in elections, and had served in World War II. He was still considered an outsider, and the CBS brass didn't think the American public was ready to accept anything other than a white, American-born man (such as Lucy's radio husband, Richard Denning) as a husband to Lucille Ball. Boy, were they wrong.

ARNAZ FAMILY
PHOTO, 1955

DESI'S SON WAS FOURTH IN LINE FOR THE NAME OF DESIDERIO ARNAZ. DESI'S PARENTS ARE ALSO SEEN IN THIS FAMILY PHOTO.

When Lucy and Desi took their show on the road to rave reviews throughout the country in 1950, they finally convinced the CBS chiefs that the U.S. viewing public had no trouble accepting them as a husband-and-wife team, much like others of their day, including George Burns and Gracie Allen. At first they wanted to play down Desi's Cuban heritage, but it soon became obvious to the writers that it was a gem and inspired countless memorable moments. When Ricky Ricardo loses his famous Latin temper and yells at his wife in Spanish, it makes you laugh, even if you don't know what he is actually saying. Also, the other characters, especially Lucy, could make fun of his cute little language mix-ups and tendencies to say words like "splain" and "sperienced."

Another aspect the sponsors (namely Philip Morris) and CBS did not want as part of the show was Desi's music. They felt that having him sing Cuban songs like his signature "Babalu" would be a turn off to the American viewing audience, but actually Desi Arnaz and his orchestra had been a hit in the New York nightclub scene for years, where they introduced the Conga. They had performed all over the country and were heard on many radio shows. In 1946, Desi even became the musical director on Bob Hope's enormously popular radio show. He was well known and his music was well liked. Since Ricky Ricardo was a bandleader, the Mertzes had been in vaudeville, and Lucy was constantly trying to break into show biz, it made perfect sense to make shows centered on performing. Hence Desi, as Ricky, sang the Latin songs he knew and had made famous.

I Love Lucy quickly became a top-ten hit and the "controversy" surrounding Desi's heritage abruptly ended. In fact, by episode three ("Be a Pal") they were already referencing his Latin roots when Lucy tries to recreate his homeland in their living room. Ricky sang more and more

DESI ARNAZ BUILT A TELEVISION EMPIRE IN THE 1950s.

songs in Spanish as the series went on, and the first episode of season two has him cooking his signature dish, *arroz con pollo* (chicken with rice).

In later episodes Ricky's Cuban friends and his mother visit him, and Spanish is spoken and translated into English. Indeed, when Mama Ricardo arrives to see her grandson for the first time, Lucy attempts to converse with her, and when that fails she employs a bilingual friend to help her appear to understand and speak the language through a microphone and earpiece contraption. It was important for her to be able to communicate with her mother-in-law and to show her respect by at least pretending to be able to speak with her. In the sixth season, they all visit Cuba and Little Ricky is able to speak perfect Spanish with his relatives. Lucy causes trouble as usual, but by the fade out she is accepted with open arms by her Cuban family.

It's important to note that there is never an *I Love Lucy* episode or even scene in which Ricky's heritage works against him. He is never discriminated against, or turned down for a position or a club membership due to his Cuban roots. In real life that was not always the case for Desi Arnaz. On the show though, Ricky's Latin identity oftentimes works in his favor, such as when he lands the role of Don Juan in a movie or when his Latin band is sent on tour to bring their particular sound to Europe. Everyone accepts Ricky, as a husband, father, businessman, best friend, tenant, and home and nightclub owner. This fact, although probably an unconscious omission by the writers, is actually very culturally significant. It helped teach equality by example to every fan of the show across America.

The importance of Desi Arnaz, as an actor, producer, writer, musician, and businessman cannot be overlooked among the pantheon of Latin-American performers in this country. Many current Latino and Latina entertainers mention him as being influential in their lives and careers. To immigrants new to this country, being able to see Desi as Ricky on television must have been very comforting. To have proof that if he could do it all, and be successful at so many things, was, and is, a credit to Desi as an entertainer, as a businessman, and as a friend, husband, and father. He was truly a groundbreaker in many ways, and the American culture has much for which to thank him.

OUR PRESIDENT and VICE PRESIDENT

"California, Here We Come!"

...JAN 10...They're Off!
...JAN 17...Room Service.
...JAN 24...Tennessee Ernie Re-visited
...JAN 31...A Star is Born?
...FEB 7...Bill Holden, Look to Your Laurels!

The Ricardos and the Mertzes packed up for a cross-country road trip to California.

During part of their extended stay in California, Lucy, Fred, and Ethel formed the Ricky Ricardo fan club.

The Mertzes plan their return to New York via motorcycle.

A look at the set for the interior of the train in "The Great Train Robbery."

On the Road with Lucy, Ricky, Fred, and Ethel

I Love Lucy was probably the first television sitcom to use travel as a major plot devise. The writers used almost every possible mode of transportation in the episodes, including automobile, ship, train, ferry, bus, bicycle, subway, fishing boat, helicopter, horseback, and airplane. Travel added many possibilities for storylines.

The idea of having the gang go out of town for an extended period of time actually emerged due to a lack of plausible new ideas from the writers. They felt that they had placed the Ricardos and Mertzes in almost every imaginable situation at home in New York. They had switched work roles, performed in shows, taken jobs as Martians, gotten arrested, tried their luck at a couple of businesses, played sports, and even gone back to the turn of the century! The show was number one in the country, but the writers felt

it was time for a change, so they decided that Ricky would get a role in a movie and be sent off to Hollywood to make a motion picture. The fact that Lucy and Desi had so many Hollywood friends made it a perfect vehicle to get some of their famous pals on the show to liven things up.

The entire fourth season was dedicated to the California trip. First Ricky had to get the part, then they had to prepare by planning, buying a car, and packing, then there were several episodes about the journey itself, and the rest of the season centered on their time in Hollywood. Of course, this was great for the viewing public as well, because it allowed them to learn more about Hollywood, and to see some of their favorite movie stars on the small screen. The gang traveled all around the area and mentioned tourist sites like Grauman's Chinese Theatre, the Hollywood Bowl, Knott's

TRAVEL BY RAIL PROVED HAZARDOUS WHEN LUCY GOT EMERGENCY BREAK HAPPY.

THE GANG WAS IN CALIFORNIA SO LONG THAT THEIR FRIENDS IN NEW YORK WELCOMED THEM (OR AT LEAST NEW STAR RICKY) WITH A GRAND HOMECOMING.

Berry Farm, Catalina Island, and the Coconut Grove. They even took a little trip down to Palm Springs (where Lucy and Desi owned a vacation home). They took a bus ride to see the homes of the stars (including a peek at the actual home of the Arnaz family on Roxbury Drive). All in all it was a wonderful break from New York, and of course it gave Lucy a chance to make trouble in another corner of the world, as well!

them packing, and Fred was hired as Ricky's band manager, so it made sense for the Mertzes to go along for the ride. This time they traveled all over the European continent—to England, France, Italy, Switzerland, and Monte Carlo. Lucy even went to Scotland in a dream! They met Queen Elizabeth II in London, got arrested in Paris, rode bikes through Italy, got caught in a landslide in Lucerne, and gambled in Monte Carlo. Even the voyage over was a story

Lucy, being Lucy, had to charter a helicopter to lower her down onto the *S.S. Constitution*.

Behind the scenes of "Bon Voyage"

The hazards of travel by ship—getting stuck in a porthole.

Traveling by bicycle across the Italian border (well, trying to, at least).

The Hollywood segment actually lasted into the fifth season, at which time the gang headed home by train. The trip had been so successful ratings wise though, that the writers decided to send them all off again, this time to Europe. Once again, it would be Ricky's career that sent

when Lucy missed the ship and had to fly out by helicopter to meet it!

When they returned from Europe at the end of season five, it was time to send them off again, almost immediately, this time to Florida and Cuba. The trip down was exciting

The gang returned home from Europe by plane.

Little Ricky gets in on the traveling
act, going by plane to Cuba.

A STOP TO CHANGE THE TIRE ON THE ROAD TO FLORIDA.

enough when Lucy and Ethel had to change a tire, escape a would-be axe murderer, and hitch a ride on a poultry wagon! Later the gang went deep-sea fishing and got stranded on what they thought was a deserted island. And then, since Cuba is so close to Florida, and Ricky (not to mention Desi) was Cuban by birth, the writers decided to send them all off to Cuba for a Ricardo family reunion.

Of course, none of these trips actually took place. All the Hollywood, Europe, Florida, and Cuba episodes were shot on set, and footage of some of the cities they visited was added in later. The actors already lived in the Hollywood area, and some of those sites were filmed so that pictures of signs, buildings, and marquees could be incorporated during the editing process. And as much as they would have all loved to travel to Europe to shoot those episodes, there was simply no reason to. They found it could all be done at home.

Even after they returned from Florida and Cuba in the sixth season, the writers made a more final travel plan when they moved them all out of New York to the Connecticut countryside. Once again, storylines were at the root of the change, as the move itself and the subsequent new potential problems for Lucy were necessary as far as the writers were

STRANGER THINGS HAVE HAPPENED ON A SUBWAY; LUCY TOOK A MEMORABLE TRIP BENEATH THE CITY IN "LUCY AND THE LOVING CUP."

concerned. After all, Lucy had created all the mayhem she could in New York, California, Florida, Cuba, and throughout Europe. It was about time another place got a taste of what she could dish out.

Advertising travel options of the day, by car, plane, and bus:

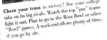

Cheer your team to victory! See your college take on its big rivals. Watch the top "pro" teams fight it out. Plan to go to the Rose Bowl or other "Bowl" games. A week-end allows plenty of time, if you go by air.

The best hunting in America—and the best fishing—are only hours away by air. On a one-week holiday you could have nine days of sport; leave on a Friday night, return on a Sunday night. You can take 40 pounds of luggage free.

Go home for the holidays. Big, modern DC6 airplanes can whisk you across the entire continent in less than half a day! Flying makes it possible for you to attend faraway weddings, graduations, anniversaries and other family events.

"Faraway" Fun — that flying makes possible!

A big time in the big city is easy to arrange—if you use the airlines. Flying gives you more time for pleasure in the city you're visiting . . . or lets you return home sooner. What's more, the trip is so short you don't have time to get tired and mussed.

WORLD'S MOST MODERN AIRPLANE. Today, 79% of Douglas production is military. But the new DC6's are being built for the airlines, too. The Douglas DC-6, most modern civilian airplane in the skies today, has carried over 20 million people on these leading airlines of the world!

Visit summer this winter. By air, you're beaches! For free, expert help in plannin below. Or see a travel agent; look under phone book.

Twice as many people fly DOUG...
AS ALL OTHER AIRPL...

AA Argentina • AMERICAN U.S. • BCPA Australian New Zealand
BRANIFF U.S. • CMA Mexican • CONTINENTAL U.S. • CPAL Canadian
DELTA U.S. • FLYING TIGER U.S. • KLM Netherlands • LAI Italian
NATIONAL U.S. • PAL Philippine • PANAGRA U.S. • PAN AMERICAN U.S.
SABENA Belgian • SAS Danish Norwegian Swedish • SLICK U.S. • SWISSAIR Swiss
• TAI French • UNITED U.S. • WESTERN U.S.

WORLD'S LARGEST BUILDER OF AIRCRAFT FOR 32 YEARS • MILITARY AND COMMERCIAL TRANSPORTS • FIGHTERS • ATTACK PLANES • BOMBER...

New beauty...

Shattering the barrier...

between thought and action with instant power for instant response

from your car! Here is complete driver-control, ...ling the toughest of all world records with ease, ...the car that amazed Indianapolis Motor Speedway ...AA officials, 2157 miles in 24 hours . . . without ...ement of engine or transmission parts . . . to win ...evens Challenge Trophy for stock car endurance! ...an exact duplicate of the car that won the Stevens ...y for the most exciting of all motoring experiences, ...a Chrysler and learn the difference!

...TIFUL CHRYSLER

10 miles...or 10,000 miles...

GATES 1-2-3 LOCAL SCHEDULES

GATE

GATES 4-5-6 THROUGH SCHEDULES

TRAVEL BUREAU

Greyhound's Your Best Buy in Travel!

BEST BUY in little trips for everyday needs!

With more schedules to more places than any other transportation, Greyhound saves you time on so many trips—gets you to the heart of downtown for business, shopping, or shows—back the same day • Convenient "mainline" service connects smaller towns and communities with all the great cities • No driving strain, no parking problems, no weather worries • Above all, little trips by Greyhound add up to **big savings!**

BEST BUY in trips to all America . . . with direct THRU-GREYHOUND service!

Greyhound offers more Through Buses (without change of coach or baggage) . . . more Express and Limited Schedules . . . more optional scenic routes than any other travel system . . . Liberal stop-over privileges, if you wish, for sightseeing, visiting • Enjoy Greyhound's high standard of service and dependability, traveling to any of the 48 States, Canada, or Mexico.

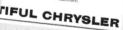

There's something about a GREYHOUND that makes it the FRIENDLY way to travel

G R E Y H O U N D

PLANNING A SPRING TRIP OR VACATION?
Mail this coupon to Greyhound Information Center, 105 W. Madison, Chicago 2, Ill. for free booklet describing 40 personally planned pleasure trips to big cities, resorts, National Parks.

Name
Address
City & State

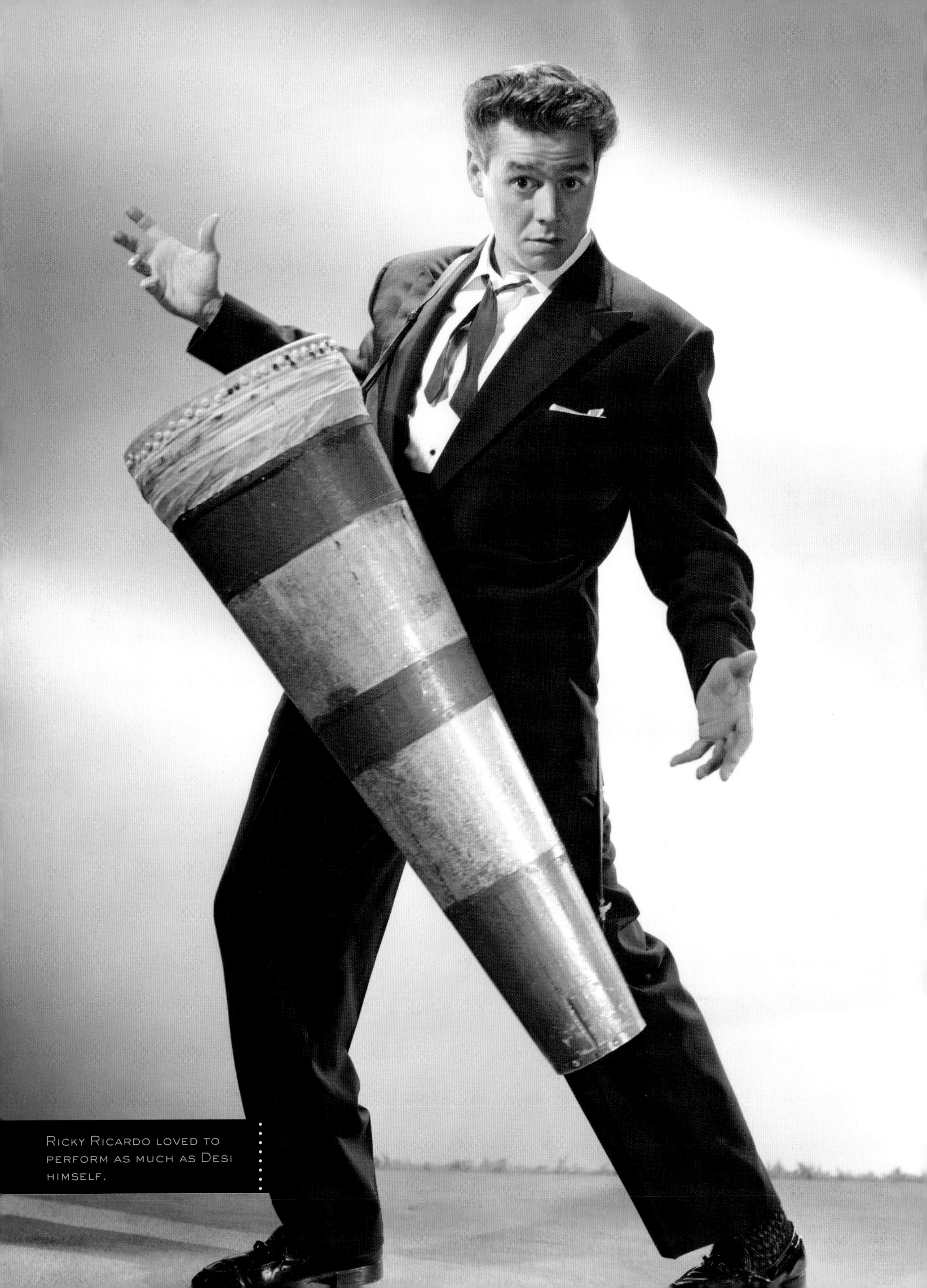

Ricky Ricardo loved to perform as much as Desi himself.

The Soundtrack of I Love Lucy

Music played a vital role on *I Love Lucy*. First of all, one of the main characters was a musician. He worked in a nightclub and made his living singing, dancing, and leading an orchestra. That same profession took him and the gang to Hollywood and to Europe. Secondly, Lucy and the Mertzes were always trying to break into the act. Ethel and Fred had been vaudevillians, and often broke into song when there was the possibility of landing a job. Lucy constantly wanted to prove her skill on the saxophone, and everyone was forever complaining about her singing voice (or lack thereof). And finally, there was Little Ricky who, like his daddy, was a drumming aficionado, and could sing "Babalu" better than any other American five-year-old.

Many *I Love Lucy* episodes were enhanced by the inclusion of music. Musical plots include: Lucy and twin-boy terrors singing while a frog is let loose from a box and ends up down Lucy's shirt; Lucy and Ethel writing and performing an operetta; numerous shows at the club; Lucy's Scottish nightmare; Ricky singing to a pregnant Lucy when he finds out they're 'specting; Mr. Livermore tippy-toeing through his garden; the Friends of the Friendless; Lucy and Ethel singing "Friendship"; Tennessee Ernie and his Hot Chicken Pickers; and doing a living room tango. So many of the episodes depended on music to move the plot along, that it would not have been feasible, or nearly as funny, had music not played an enormous part in the show.

Desi brought the distinct sounds of African, Cuban, and Spanish music to an America that had, for the most part, not experienced anything like it right in their living rooms. It would be decades before Gloria Estefan and the Miami Sound Machine, Carlos Santana, and Jennifer Lopez would be commonplace on radio throughout the country. Before that could occur, American audiences would be introduced to Elvis Presley, Chuck Berry, the Beatles, and the Rolling Stones.

171

It's interesting to note that before the show was even picked up by Philip Morris, no one wanted Desi to sing at all. The story goes that there was a meeting of representatives of the Biow advertising agency and Philip Morris, at which famed musician Oscar Hammerstein was present. After viewing the pilot episode, Hammerstein reportedly said they should keep the redhead but get rid of the Cuban. When it was explained that the couple was a package deal, Hammerstein advised that at the very least they should not allow Desi to sing on the show. How different it would have been if they had listened to him.

"California, Here I Come!"

. . . .

By B.G. Desylva, Al Jolson, and Joseph Meyer

. . . .

Sung in "California, Here I Come!"

When the wintry wind starts blowing
And the snow is starting in a fall
Then my eyes went westward knowing
That's the place that I love best of all
California, I've been blue
Since I've been away from you
I can't wait till I get blowing
Even now I'm starting in a call

California, here I come
Right back where I started from
Where bowers of flowers bloom in the spring
Each morning at dawning birdies sing at everything
A sun-kissed miss said, "Don't be late!"
That's why I can hardly wait
Open up that golden gate
California, here I come

California, here I come, yeah

Right back where I started from

Where bowers of flowers bloom in the spring

Each morning at dawning birdies sing at everything

A sun-kissed miss said, "Don't be late!"

That's why I can hardly wait, come on, come on

Open up, open up, open up that golden gate

California, here I come

"Ricochet (Rick-O-Shay)"

By Larry Coleman, Joe Darion, and Norman Gimbel

Sung in "Tennessee Bound"

They warned me when you kissed me, your love would ricochet

Your lips would find another, and your heart would go astray

I thought that I could hold you with all my many charms

But then one day you ricocheted to someone else's arms

And baby

I don't want a ricochet romance,

I don't want a ricochet love

If you're careless with your kisses,

Find another turtle dove

I can't live on ricochet romance, no, no not me

If you're gonna ricochet, baby,

I'm gonna set you free!

I knew the day I met you, you had a rovin' eye

I thought that I could hold you, what a fool I was to try

You promised you'd be faithful, and you would never stray

Then like a rifle bullet, you began to ricochet

And baby

I don't want a ricochet romance,

I don't want a ricochet love

If you're careless with your kisses,

Find another turtle dove

I can't live on ricochet romance, no, no not me

If you're gonna ricochet, baby,

I'm gonna set you free!

When you announced our wedding, you made me mighty proud

I whispered "Two was company" but you preferred a crowd

You buzzed around the other girls just like a busy bee

And when you finished buzzin', cousin, you buzzed right back to me

And baby

I don't want a ricochet romance,

I don't want a ricochet love

If you're careless with your kisses,

Find another turtle dove

I can't live on ricochet romance, no, no not me

If you're gonna ricochet, baby,

I'm gonna set you free!

They popped up well and started to sing
Skipping 'round the room doing the pigeon wing

Mamma's little baby loves shortnin', shortnin'
Mamma's little baby loves shortnin' bread
Mamma's little baby loves shortnin', shortnin'
Mamma's little baby loves shortnin' bread

Put on the skillet
Put on the lid
Mamma's going to make some shortnin' bread
That's not all she's going to do
Mamma's going to cook us some cocoa too

Mamma's little baby loves shortnin', shortnin'
Mamma's little baby loves shortnin' bread
Mamma's little baby loves shortnin', shortnin'
Mamma's little baby loves shortnin' bread

I snuck to the kitchen, picked up the lid
I filled my pockets full of shortnin' bread
I winked at the pretty little girl and said

"Shortnin' Bread"

Sung in "Ethel's Hometown"

Mamma's little baby loves shortnin', shortnin'
Mamma's little baby loves shortnin' bread
Mamma's little baby loves shortnin', shortnin'
Mamma's little baby loves shortnin' bread

Three little children layin' in the bed
Two were sick and the other 'most dead
Sent for the doctor, the doctor said
"Feed those children on shortnin' bread"

Mamma's little baby loves shortnin', shortnin'
Mamma's little baby loves shortnin' bread
Mamma's little baby loves shortnin', shortnin'
Mamma's little baby loves shortnin' bread

When those children layin' in the bed
Heard that talk about shortnin' bread

"Baby, how'd you like some shortnin' bread"

Mamma's little baby loves shortnin', shortnin'
Mamma's little baby loves shortnin' bread
Mamma's little baby loves shortnin', shortnin'
Mamma's little baby loves shortnin' bread

Got caught with the skillet
Got caught with the lid
Got caught with my mouth full of shortnin' bread
Six months for the skillet, six months for the lid
Six months in the jail eatin' shortnin' bread

Mamma's little baby loves shortnin', shortnin'
Mamma's little baby loves shortnin' bread
Mamma's little baby loves shortnin', shortnin'
Mamma's little baby loves shortnin' bread.

Since twenty-first century people probably don't know what Shortnin' Bread is, here is an explanation:

Shortnin' bread is a treat that the early American cooks working on the plantations in the South could whip up easily with ingredients that were readily available: butter, brown sugar, and flour. Shortnin' bread is actually shortbread, which is a type of cookie that has been popular for hundreds of years in the British Isles. The difference is that in the pre-war southern United States, the shortbread was made with brown sugar. The brown sugar gives the shortnin' bread a distinctive and wonderful flavor.

"This delicious treat is the subject of the children's folk song, "Shortnin' Bread." It is unknown who wrote the lyrics, but it is widely believed that the song originated among the slaves working on the plantations in the South in the early 1800s. The actual words to the song as well as the order of the verses can vary. However, the point of the song is that a doctor orders shortnin' bread to be given to two sick children, and they are healed after eating it.

This recipe for shortnin' bread, which was adapted from a recipe featured in *Princess Pamela's Soul Food Cookbook* (Signet 1969), is made easily because the dough is simply patted down in a jellyroll pan, then immediately cut into squares and served while warm.

Ingredients

2 cups butter

1 cup brown sugar

4 cups flour

½ teaspoon salt

Directions

In a large bowl, cream the butter and sugar until very light and fluffy. Mix the flour and salt; turn the mixer down to slow speed and add it to the creamed butter mixture, mixing until fully incorporated.

Transfer the dough to a parchment-lined jellyroll pan and press until it is smooth and even. Using a sharp knife and a ruler, score the dough into squares, or triangles. Bake at 325°F for 25 minutes or until golden brown. Immediately use a sharp knife to cut through the score marks. Cool thoroughly before serving.

Store the baked shortbread in an airtight container; it will keep for several weeks. It may also be wrapped tightly and frozen for several months.

"My Hero"

By Oscar Straus, Rudolph Bernauer, and Leopold Jacobson; English lyrics by Stanislaus Stange

Sung in "Ethel's Hometown"

I have a true and noble lover

He is my sweetheart, all my own

His like on Earth, who shall discover

My heart is his and his alone

We pledged our troth each to the other

And for our happiness, I pray

Our lives belong to one another

Oh, happy, happy wedding day

Oh, happy, happy wedding day

Come, come, I love you only

My heart is true

Come, come, my life is lonely

I long for you

Come, come, naught can efface you

My arms are aching now to embrace you

You are divine

Come, come, I love you only

Come, hero mine

"Mama Yo Quiero"

By Jararaca Paiva and Emilio Vincente de Torre

Sung in "Be a Pal"

Mamãe eu quero, mamãe eu quero

Mamãe eu quero mama!

Dá a chupeta, ai, dá a chupeta

Dá a chupeta pro bebê não chorar!

Dorme filhinho do meu coração

Pega a mamadeira e vem entra no meu cordão

Eu tenho uma irmã que se chama Ana

De piscar o olho já ficou sem a pestana

Eu olho as pequenas, mas daquele jeito

E tenho muita pena não ser criança de peito

Eu tenho uma irmã que é fenomenal

Ela é da bossa e o marido é um boçal

"Cuban Pete"

. . . .

By Jose Norman

. . . .

Sung in "The Diet," "The Hedda Hopper Story," "Lucy Goes to a Rodeo"

They raved about Sloppy Joe,

The Latin Lothario,

But Havana has a new sensation

He's really a modest guy,

Although he's the hottest guy in Havana

And here's what he has to say:

They call me Cuban Pete

I'm the king of the Rhumba beat

When I play the maracas I go

Chick-chickee boom, chick-chickee boom, chick-chickee boom

Yes, sir, I'm Cuban Pete,

I'm the craze of my native street

When I start to dance, everything goes

Chick-chickee boom, chick-chickee boom, chick-chickee boom

The señoritas they sing and how they swing

With this rhumbero

It's very nice, so full of spice

And when they're dancin' they bring a happy ring

Never a care—oh!

Singin' a song, all the day long

So if you like the beat

Take a lesson from Cuban Pete

And I'll teach you to

Chick-chickee boom, chick-chickee boom, chick-chickee boom

Si, señorita, I know that you will like

The chickee boom, chick,

'Cause it's the dance

Of Latin romance

And Cuban Pete doesn't teach you

In a hurry like Arthur Murray,

You're now in Havana,

And there's always mañana

So, señorita, please,

Take it easy, do it with ease,

And you'll love it when you do

The chick-chickee boom, chick-chickee boom

Chick-chick-chick-chick-chickee boom, chick-chickee boom

Chick-chickee boom . . .

"Cuban Cabby"

By Nat Simon, James Cavanaugh, and John Redmond

Sung in "The Club Election"

My horse and carriage is for hire, Señor

For just as long as you desire, Señor

You want to ride?

Forget the mañana and come to Havana with me

I'm the Cuban Cabby. I'm the Cuban Cabby.

The taxi drivers drive you frantic, you know

Oh, but, my rig is more romantic and so,

You want to ride?

An eye full of splendor and you can depend upon me

I'm the Cuban Cabby and I need dinero

(Money, that is)

The moon is peeping, the shadows creeping

It's time for riding through the park

A lovely night for lovers. The same as you two are.

If you like music, I'll give you music as we go riding in the dark

I'll sing a Spanish love song to the strains of my guitar

My horse and carriage is for hire, Señor

For just as long as you desire, Señor

You want to ride?

The sweet señoritas and gay caballeros know me

I'm the Cuban Cabby, and I know my business,

And I mind my business.

You want to ride? (The Cuban Cabby)

You want to ride? (Will make you happy)

You want to ride?

"Babalu"

By Margarita Lecuona

Sung in "The Audition," "The Young Fans," "The Publicity Agent," "Lucy Hires an English Tutor," "Ricky's _LIFE_ Story," "The Ricardos Visit Cuba"

Babalu

Babalu

Babalu aye

Babalu aye

Babalu

'Ta empezando lo velorio

Y que le hacemo a Babalu

Dame diez y siete velas

Pa' ponerle en cruz

Dame un cabo de tabaco mayenye

Y un jarrito de aguardiente

Dame un poco de dinero mayenye

Pa' que me de la suerte

Yo quiero pedi'

Que me negra me quiere

Que tenga dinero

Y que no se muera

Ay! Vo le quiero pedi' a Babalu 'na negra muy santa como tu que no tenga otro negro

Pa' que no se fuera.

Babalu a ye! (Repeat ten times)

"El Cumbanchero"

....

By Rafael Hernandez

....

Sung in "Breaking the Lease"

El cumba, cumba, cumba, cumbanchero

El bongo, bongo, bongo, bongosero

Priquiti que va sonando

El cumbanchero, bongosero que se va

Bongsero que se va

El cumba, cumba, cumba, cumbanchero

El bongo, bongo, bongo, bongosero

Priquiti que va sonando

El cumbanchero, bongosero que se va

Bongsero que se va

E suena ciel tambor priquiti

Boom boom boom boom boom boom ba!

Y vielvia repicar priquiti

Boom boom boom boom boom boom ba!

El cumba, cumba, cumba, cumbanchero

El bongo, bongo, bongo, bongosero

Priquiti que va sonando

El cumbanchero, bongosero que se va

Bongsero que se va

RICKY SINGS "THERE'S A BRAND NEW BABY
AT OUR HOUSE" IN "SALES RESISTANCE."

"I'll See You in C-U-B-A"

. . . .

By Irving Berlin

. . . .

Sung in "The Ricardos Visit Cuba"

Not so far from here

There's a very lively atmosphere

Everybody's going there this year

And there's a reason . . .

The season never closes there

Love and music you'll find everywhere

People always havin' fun down there

So come along.

I'm on my way to Cuba

That's where I'm goin'

Cuba, that's where I'll stay

Cuba, where wine is flowin'

Where dark-eyed stellas

Light their fellas Panatellas.

Cuba, where all is happy

Cuba, where all is gay.

Why don't you plan a wonderful trip

To Havana, hop on a ship,

And I'll see you in C-U-B-A!

Why don't you plan a wonderful trip

To Havana, hop on a ship,

And I'll see you,

I'll see you,

Yes, I'll see you in C-U-B-A!

"We're Having a Baby"

. . . .

By Desi Arnaz

. . . .

Sung in "Lucy is Enceinte"

We're having a baby, my baby and me

You'll read it in Winchell's

That we're adding a limb to our family tree

While pushing our carriage

How proud I will be

There's nothing like marriage

Ask your mother and father and they'll agree.

He'll have toys, baby clothes

He'll know he's come to the right house

By and by, when he grows

Maybe he'll live in the White House

Our future gets brighter

But definitely

We're having a baby

We're having a baby

We're having a baby

My baby and me

"There's a Brand New Baby at Our House"

By Desi Arnaz (written for his daughter, Lucie)

Sung in "Sales Resistance"

There's a brand new baby at our house

The nicest little gift we've ever had

How much fuller life's become

No one knows what makes it hum

'Til you call each other mommy and dad

There's a brand new baby at our house

And though she's been there just a little while

In the parlor in the hall

Every picture on the wall

Seems to know because they all wear a smile

I can't explain what she does to my heart

With her infant charms

I never knew what heaven was

'Til I held an angel in my arms

There's a brand new baby at our house

She's twice as sweet as honey from the comb

She's the image of my spouse

She's the tricky Mickey Mouse

Who has changed our happy house to a home

We thank the Lord

Whose love and wondrous powers

Gave us the brand new

Grand new

Baby of ours

"Friendship"

By Cole Porter

Sung in "Lucy and Ethel Buy the Same Dress"

If you're ever in a jam, here I am

If you're ever in a mess, S-O-S

If you ever feel so happy, you land in jail; I'm your bail.

It's friendship, friendship, just a perfect blendship.

When other friendships have been forgot,

Ours will still be hot.

Lah-dle-ah-dle-ah-dle dig, dig, dig.

If you're ever up a tree, phone to me.

If you're ever down a well, ring my bell.

If you ever lose your teeth, and you're out to dine; borrow mine.

It's friendship, friendship, just a perfect blendship.

When other friendships have been forgate,

Ours will still be great.

Lah-dle-ah-dle-ah-dle, chuck, chuck, chuck.

If they ever black your eyes, put me wise.

If they ever cook your goose, turn me loose.

If they ever put a bullet through your brain; I'll complain.

It's friendship, friendship, just a perfect blendship.

When other friendships have been forgit,

Ours will still be it.

Lah-dle-ah-dle-ah-dle, hep, hep, hep.

"I Love Lucy"

....

By Harold Adamson

....

Sung in "Lucy's Last Birthday"

I love Lucy and she loves me,

We're as happy as two can be.

Sometimes we quarrel but then,

How we love making up again.

Lucy kisses like no one can,

She's my missus and I'm her man.

And life is Heaven you see,

'Cause I love Lucy, yes, I love Lucy

And Lucy loves me!

"Y'all Come"

....

The original song was written by Bill Monroe, but Desilu and Ernie Ford added special lyrics in the last verse to celebrate Cousin Ernie's visit.

....

Sung in "Tennessee Ernie Hangs On"

When you live in the country everybody is your neighbor

Of this one thing you can rely—slap my thigh.

They all come to see you, and they never leave you

Saying y'all come to see us by and by.

By and by, by and by.

Y'all come

Y'all come

Oh, you all come to see us when you can (it's for free)

Y'all come (bring the pigs), y'all come (ah ha)

Oh, you all come to see us now and then.

Kin folks are a comin', they're comin' by the dozen

Eating everything from soup to hay

Hi, cousin!

And right after dinner

They ain't looking any thinner,

And here's what you hear them say:

Y'all come (bring the kids), y'all come (land a Goshen)

Oh, you all come to see us when you can

Y'all come, y'all come

Oh, you all come to see us now and then.

Jim and June and Uncle Andy, Cousin Pete, and Aunt Mirandi,

All the cows and chickens, too.

Jim and June can sip some cider, Ma and Pa can ride the glider

Cousin Rick can yodel "Babalu" (Babalu)

Y'all come

Y'all come

Oh, you all come to see us when you can

Y'all come, y'all come

Oh, you all come to see us now and then.

LUCY IN HER POOLSIDE BEST. "IN PALM SPRINGS"

On Fashion

As much as she tried, Lucy Ricardo was not a woman one would consider a fashion plate. Like most women of her era, age, and economic status, Lucy tried hard to keep up with the Joneses. She was constantly shopping for hats and gowns, and nagging Ricky to buy her a fur coat. Quite often her clothing expenditures got her into trouble with her hubby, but somehow she always managed to get what she wanted.

When *I Love Lucy* first started and for the first two seasons, there was no real costume department except for Lucy's wardrobe mistress, Della Fox. All actors were asked to bring in their own clothing from home, and even Desi Arnaz wore his own suits, shoes, and ties on the show. Since there wasn't a large budget for costuming, Lucy Ricardo's dresses were all either purchased at Ohrbach's department store, or sewn by dressmakers from a couple of simple dress patterns. The details of each dress were changed slightly from time to time to make sure the dresses did not look exactly alike. This

actually made sense for the Lucy character because Lucy Ricardo was a middle-class housewife who would not be wearing *haute couture* (except, of course, when she shopped at Don Loper's salon, or Jacques Marcel's Parisian boutique!).

In 1953, Desilu hired Academy Award-winning designer Elois Jenssen to design Lucy Ricardo's clothing. Elois set up a costume department with sewing machines and bolts of fabric from which she created some of the show's most recognizable outfits. Elois designed some memorable clothing for Lucy, including the matching gowns she and Vivian wore, their "charm school" evening dresses, Lucy's famous flowing sheer black housecoat, the dress she wore when she fell in the starch vat, and all the clothing for their trip to Hollywood. In the fifth season, Edward Stevenson replaced Elois Jenssen, and continued in the position of designer until the show ended in 1960. He helped design the clothing worn in Lucy's Scottish dream (including

the two-headed dragon), and the burlap sack dresses she and Ethel wore on the streets of Paris.

The end of World War II influenced change in the clothing of the 1950s. In America, although not in Europe, gone were restrictions and rationing on clothing. No longer did families have to mend all their clothing and "make do" with what they had. The patriotic "uniform" look for women had gone, along with the popularity of headscarves, which had served practical purposes for those involved with factory war work. Most women and girls had knitted in their spare time, and knitted socks and sweaters helped keep the home front warm during the heat rationing of the war. Stockings, a luxury during the war (women wore ankle socks or drew seams up the backs of their legs when they had no stockings), were no longer a scarcity.

Fashion designers such as Christian Dior and Gabrielle "Coco" Chanel were all the rage during the post-war years. In 1953 Dior launched his "Princess" line and popularized A-line skirts. Chanel presented collarless jackets with matching skirts. Skirts and dresses, which had been shorter and narrow, became longer and fuller after the war. Accents like buttons, ribbon, and braid came back into style, and feathers were wildly popular. Knee-length coats were seen on many women, as were loose, full sleeves. Silk was back in vogue. So was the "status symbol" of fur, used on collars and wrists, as well as for coats and jackets. Leopard prints were seen on fashionable women, and Ethel Mertz even wore such a gown in an *I Love Lucy* episode. In direct contrast to the aforementioned feminine frills, slacks for women also became increasingly popular.

For men, tweed was in, as were gray flannel suits, tuxedos, polo shirts, cardigans, patterns, and comfortable loafers. For teens it was all about poodle skirts and jeans, saddle shoes, and penny loafers.

When it came to accessories, both men and women wore hats when they left the house, and women often wore their hats in the house when they were visiting. Another necessity for women were gloves, and no self-respecting housewife would be caught dead in the kitchen without an apron.

On *I Love Lucy*, wacky fashions abounded. In many episodes the cast wore wild clothing or costumes when they put on shows. Lucy's well-known polka dot dress was seen often, as was the long black housecoat, paired with ballet flats. Some shows were even built around clothing, such as Lucy wanting a fur coat or buying yet another hat. Since *I Love Lucy* is known and remembered in part by its array of crazy costumes, following is a guide to the more memorable get-ups seen in the show.

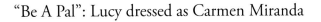

"Be A Pal": Lucy dressed as Carmen Miranda

"The Diet": Lucy squeezed into the sequined "Sally Sweet" number

"The Audition": Lucy dressed as "The Professor" in her loose-fitting tuxedo

"The Séance": Ethel dressed as Madame Mertzola

"Men Are Messy": Lucy dressed as a country bumpkin

"The Fur Coat": the first time we hear Lucy wish for a fur

"Lucy is Jealous of Girl Singer": Lucy dresses up as a chorus girl

"The Benefit": Lucy and Ricky in matching striped suits

"The Amateur Hour": Lucy and the twins in cowboy garb

"Lucy Plays Cupid": Miss Ritter in an 1890s dress, and Lucy

looking like a character out of *The Grapes of Wrath*

"Lucy Writes a Play": Lucy, Ethel, and Ricky dressed up for the stage

"The Ballet": Lucy in a tutu, not to mention dressed as a burlesque comic

"New Neighbors": Lucy as an easy chair

"Fred and Ethel Fight": Lucy bandaged from head to toe

"The Moustache": Lucy dressed like Colonel Sanders, complete with facial hair

"Pioneer Women": the whole gang dressed in styles from 1900

"The Marriage License": Lucy in her wedding dress

"The Kleptomaniac": Lucy as a gangster

"Cuban Pals": Lucy's costume for "African Wedding Dance"

"Lucy Does a TV Commercial": Lucy in her famous checkered dress

"The Publicity Agent": Lucy as Princess Scheherazade, and Ethel as her handmaiden

"The Anniversary Present": Lucy and Ethel in overalls; Ricky buys pearls for Lucy

"The Operetta": the gang dressed up to perform Lucy's musical

"Job Switching": those famous uniforms from Kramer's Kandy Kitchen

"The Saxophone": Lucy as a "cool cat"

"Lucy is Enceinte": Lucy wears maternity clothing

"Lucy's Show Biz Swan Song": the gang as a barbershop quartet

"The Club Election": Lucy with bejeweled cardigan and matching handbag

"The Indian Show": the gang as Native Americans

"Lucy is Matchmaker": Lucy and Ethel in negligees

"Lucy Wants New Furniture": Lucy makes her own dress

"The Camping Trip": Lucy in hip boots and flannel

"Ricky's *LIFE* Story": Lucy as a Spanish *señorita* on a balcony

"Lucy and Ethel Buy the Same Dress": Lucy and Ethel wear the same gown on TV

"The French Revue": Lucy in a bass case, and as a French matron

"Redecorating the Mertzes' Apartment": Ricky says he will buy Lucy a fur

"Too Many Crooks": the Ricardos want to buy Fred a tweed suit

"Changing the Boys' Wardrobe": Ricky and Fred wear old, comfortable clothing

"Lucy Has Her Eyes Examined": Lucy as a bobbysoxer

"The Million-Dollar Idea": Lucy as Isabella Klump and Lucille McGillicuddy

"The Charm School": Lucy and Ethel in skin-tight gowns, Ricky as a Musketeer, and Fred looking like Winston Churchill

"Sentimental Anniversary": Ricky buys Lucy a fur wrap

"Home Movies": Lucy, Ethel, and Fred in cowboy gear

"Bonus Bucks": Lucy in a starched dressed

"Ricky's Hawaiian Vacation": Lucy, Ethel, and Fred in island attire

"Lucy is Envious": Lucy and Ethel as Martians

"Lucy's Club Dance": Ricky's (all-male) band dressed as women

"The Black Wig": Lucy as an Italian cutie and Ethel as an ethnic hybrid

"The Diner": Ethel and Fred in chef's attire

"Tennessee Ernie Hangs On": the gang and Ernie dressed as hot chicken pickers

"The Golf Game": Lucy and Ethel in plus fours and argyle socks

"Mertz and Kurtz": the gang in turn-of-the-century vaudeville costumes

"The Matchmaker": Fred in his nightgown and stocking cap, in Lucy's bed

"Mr. and Mrs. TV Show": Lucy in a burlap sack dress, knee-highs, and men's boots

"Ricky's Movie Offer": Lucy as Marilyn Monroe, and Ethel, Fred, and Mrs. Trumble looking like they just returned from Madrid

"Ethel's Birthday": Lucy buys Ethel harlequin design hostess pants

"Ricky's Contract": Lucy in her Hollywood glamour finery

"Ethel's Home Town": Lucy and the guys as they try to upstage Ethel's big moment

"L.A. at Last!": Lucy dons glasses and a fake nose to hide from William Holden

"Don Juan and the Starlets": Fred dressed as a typical Hollywood tourist

"Lucy Gets in Pictures": Lucy in feathers and tulle as a Hollywood show girl

"The Fashion Show": Lucy buys a Don Loper original, and models a tweed suit

"The Hedda Hopper Story": Lucy and Ricky get all dolled up, and all wet

"Don Juan is Shelved": Lucy, the Mertzes, and Mother McGillicuddy as Ricky's bobbysoxer fans

"Bull Fight Dance": Ricky as a matador and Lucy as Bessie the cow

"The Dancing Star": Lucy helps out Van Johnson with his dance routine in a beautiful feathered-skirt dress

"Harpo Marx": Lucy dresses like several (male) Hollywood celebrities

"Ricky Needs an Agent": Lucy in a severe corporate business suit

"The Tour": Ethel and Fred dress as hospital attendants

"Lucy and the Dummy": Lucy in her Spanish *mantilla*

"Ricky Sells the Car": the Mertzes in black leather and motorcycle boots

"Lucy Goes to a Rodeo": the gang performs as bell-ringing cowboys

"Nursery School": Lucy dresses up as a maternity case and as an operating-room nurse

"Bon Voyage": Lucy has to don coveralls to fly in a helicopter

"Lucy Meets the Queen": Lucy, dressed as a dancing horse, gets to meet Her Majesty

"The Fox Hunt": Lucy shows off her hunting pink

"Lucy Goes to Scotland": Lucy and Ricky in kilts, and Ethel and Fred as a dragon

"Lucy Gets a Paris Gown": Lucy and Ethel wear burlap on the Champs-Elysées

"Lucy in the Swiss Alps": Ethel and Fred in *lederhosen*

"Lucy's Italian Movie": Lucy as a grape-stomping peasant

"Return Home from Europe": Lucy in a baby bonnet

"Lucy and Bob Hope": Lucy as a hot-dog vendor and a baseball player

"Lucy Meets Orson Welles": Lucy in a Chinese gown

"Little Ricky Gets Stage Fright": Lucy in a Dixieland band uniform

"Visitor from Italy": Lucy dressed as a pizza chef

"The Ricardos Visit Cuba": Lucy hides out dressed as a cigar roller

"Little Ricky's School Pageant": Fred is a frog, Ricky is a tree, Ethel is a fairy queen, and Lucy is the forest witch

"*I Love Lucy* Christmas Show": everyone dresses as Santa

"Lucy and the Loving Cup": Lucy buys a new hat, but gets a trophy stuck on her head

"Lucy and Superman": Lucy tries to look like the Man of Steel

"Lucy Wants to Move to the Country": Lucy and the Mertzes dress like gangsters

"Lucy Does the Tango": Lucy stuffs her coat with three dozen eggs

"Ragtime Band": the gang dresses like a calypso group

"Country Club Dance": Lucy wears a too-tight formal dress

"The Ricardos Dedicate a Statue": Ricky and the Mertzes dress as patriots, while Lucy pretends to be a Minuteman

Dots! Dots! Dots!

Polka dots first became fashionable in late nineteenth-century Britain. Lucy Ricardo's dark dress with the white polka dots is iconic, and is recognized decades later as part of her "look." Although that dress went through many changes to its sleeves, collar, and bodice through the seasons, the basic look has stood the test of time in Lucy lore. Lucy wore a polka dot dress in more than two dozen episodes, including the final episode of the series. Along with Lucy's dress, there were several other polka-dotted items of clothing, worn by Lucy, Ethel, and Fred.

Lucy's famous polka dot dress was worn in the following episodes:

"The Quiz Show"

"The Fur Coat"

"Lucy Fakes Illness"

"Breaking the Lease"

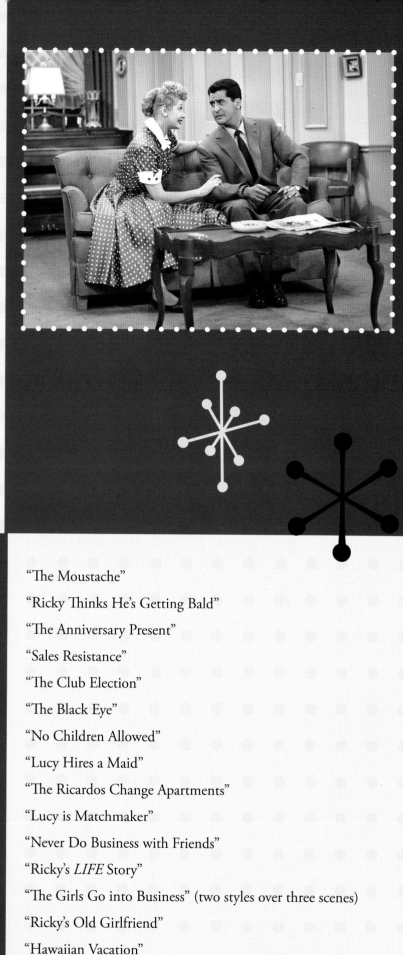

"The Moustache"

"Ricky Thinks He's Getting Bald"

"The Anniversary Present"

"Sales Resistance"

"The Club Election"

"The Black Eye"

"No Children Allowed"

"Lucy Hires a Maid"

"The Ricardos Change Apartments"

"Lucy is Matchmaker"

"Never Do Business with Friends"

"Ricky's *LIFE* Story"

"The Girls Go into Business" (two styles over three scenes)

"Ricky's Old Girlfriend"

"Hawaiian Vacation"

"Lucy Writes a Novel"

"The Diner"

"Tennessee Ernie Hangs On"

"The Sublease"

"The Homecoming"

"Lucy Meets Charles Boyer"

"Lucy Goes to Monte Carlo"

"Deep-Sea Fishing"

"Lucy and Superman"

"Country Club Dance"

"Lucy Dedicates a Statue"

"The Fashion Show" (Lucy's bathing suit)

"Don Juan is Shelved" (Lucy's underskirt and bow)

"Bull Fight Dance" (Lucy's blouse)

"The Star Upstairs" (Lucy's underskirt)

"In Palm Springs" (Lucy's blouse and Fred's tie)

"Lucy Visits Grauman's" (Lucy's underskirt and bow)

"Lucy and John Wayne" (Lucy's handkerchief)

"Ricky Sells the Car" (Lucy's underskirt and bow)

"Second Honeymoon" (Ethel's dress)

"Lucy Meets Orson Welles" (Fred's tie and Ethel's bow)

"Visitor from Italy" (Fred's tie and Ethel's bow)

"Off to Florida" (Ethel's scarf)

"Desert Island" (Ethel's dress)

"Lucy and Superman" (Fred's tie)

"Lucy Wants to Move to the Country" (Lucy's blouse and Fred's tie)

"Lucy Hates to Leave" (Lucy's blouse)

"Lucy Gets Chummy with the Neighbors" (Ethel's bow)

"Lucy Does the Tango" (Lucy's blouse)

"Building a Barbecue" (Lucy's blouse)

Polka dots were also worn in:

"The Gossip" (Lucy's apron)

"The Anniversary Present" (Grace Foster's dress)

"Lucy Hires an English Tutor" (Lucy's maternity top)

"Home Movies" (Ethel's dress)

"Bonus Bucks" (Fred's tie)

"Hawaiian Vacation" (Fred's tie)

"The Business Manager" (Fred's tie)

"Mertz and Kurtz" (Lucy and Ethel's costumes)

"Lucy Cries Wolf" (Fred's tie)

"Ethel's Birthday" (Fred's tie)

"PIONEER WOMEN"

For the Fun of It

The words, "Lucy you've got some 'splainin' to do" were never actually uttered by Ricky Ricardo, or any other character on *I Love Lucy*. He did say, "'splain that if you can!," "Lucy, 'splain," "Alright, start 'splainin'," and "There is something here that needs 'spainin'."

• There are several episodes in which Fred Mertz does not appear: "The Quiz Show," "Lucy is Jealous of Girl Singer," and "The Amateur Hour." Ethel does not appear in "The Audition" or "Lucy Does a TV Commercial," and neither of them appears in "Lucy Plays Cupid" or "Young Fans." After the first season, both Mertzes appear in every episode.

• In "Drafted," Lucy and Ethel have coffee at a table in Ethel's apartment while they knit socks and cry over their hubbies' impending enlistment. Interestingly enough, Ethel has the same china pattern that Lucy does!

• In "The Fur Coat," the gang discusses the fact that the Ricardos moved into the building on August 6, 1948. August 6th is Lucille Ball's actual birthday.

• Lucy tries to tell Ricky about her pregnancy five times before he finally figures it out for himself! By the way, the title of that episode, "Lucy is Enceinte," is so named because *enceinte* is French for "pregnant" and the writers could not use the English version of that particular word in connection with the show as it was considered indelicate.

• Lucy calls her son "the baby" throughout the series, even when he is five years old, going off to school every day, having sleepovers, and playing baseball!

• Lucy and Ethel cry together in several episodes— "Drafted," "Breaking the Lease," "Vacation from Marriage," "The Diner," "Ethel's Birthday," "Lucy in the Swiss Alps," "Desert Island," and "Lucy Wants to Move to the Country."

• In "The Séance" we learn that Ricky has five brothers and that his mother was a singer and dancer. There is no mention of his father. In "The Camping Trip" we learn that

"LUCY AND THE DUMMY"

"THE AMATEUR HOUR"

"LUCY WRITES A PLAY"

"The Ballet"

• Gregory Peck is the first movie star mentioned in *I Love Lucy*. Ethel talks about him in the very first aired episode, "The Girls Want to Go to a Nightclub."

• Both of Lucy's co-stars from her radio show *My Favorite Husband* do guest appearances on *I Love Lucy*. Bea Benadaret plays Miss Lewis in the "Lucy Plays Cupid" episode, and Gale Gordon twice plays Ricky's boss, Mr. Littlefield, in "Lucy's Schedule" and in "Ricky Asks for a Raise." Richard Denning, who played her husband on the radio, does not make a guest appearance on the TV show.

• In "Be a Pal," Lucy used DUZ soap flakes. DUZ was a product first marketed in the 1950s. It was up against another Proctor & Gamble product, Tide detergent, and its commercials appeared on the CBS radio program *The Guiding Light*, the same year that *I Love Lucy* debuted on TV. The DUZ catchphrase was, "For white washes without red hands, DUZ does everything!"

• In "Lucy Thinks Ricky is Trying to Murder Her," she throws her mystery novel out the window three times.

• The first time we learn that Lucy is no good at managing her finances is in "The Quiz Show."

• In "The Audition," Lucy makes Ricky his favorite pie—cherry.

Fred has a brother. Ethel often talks about Aunt Martha and Uncle Elmo, and Uncle Oscar and Aunt Emmie. We learn in later episodes that her father is Will Potter, but we never hear about her mother.

• In "Vacation From Marriage" we learn that the Mertz apartment building is five stories tall.

• In "Lucy's Bicycle Trip" we learn that Ricky was raised on a tobacco farm, and in an earlier episode ("Lucy is Envious") Lucy told Cynthia Harcourt that Ricky owns a sugar plantation.

• In "Lucy Writes a Novel," the Ricardo fireplace is used for the first and only time.

• In "The Diet," Lucy first claims to be a great singer and dancer. Also, this is the first time we hear her maiden name—McGillicuddy. Also in this episode we learn that she weighed 120 pounds when she married, and wore a size twelve dress.

"Lucy's Schedule"

"THE OPERETTA"

"LUCY'S SHOWBIZ SWAN SONG"

• In "Lucy is Jealous of Girl Singer," Ricky first mentions his love of *arroz con pollo* (chicken with rice).

• In "Ricky Thinks He's Getting Bald," Lucy's mirrored vanity is replaced by a chair.

• In "The Adagio" we first hear of Ethel's love of eating when she eats three pieces of cake—her limit. We also hear of Ricky's desire to move to the country, and his ability to act both jealous and macho.

• In "Men Are Messy," Ricky first utters the phrase, "Esta mujer esta absolutamente loca." (This woman is absolutely crazy!)

• "The Fur Coat" episode is the first one in which Ricky utters his famous phrase, "Lucy, I'm home!"

• In "Lucy Fakes Illness," Lucy says, "This is it, Ricky." In

"DESERT ISLAND"

"Lucy Goes to the Hospital" she utters, "Ricky, this is it."

• In "The Benefit," Lucy first asks Ricky to do her the favor of performing for a woman's club fundraiser. This time it isn't even for her club; it's for Ethel's Middle East 68th Street Woman's Club.

• The first time Lucy and Ricky met, he called her a cute little chicken. ("Ricky Thinks He's Getting Bald")

• In "Lucy Writes a Play," she stomps on the floor to call Ethel to come up to her apartment. In the very next episode, "Breaking the Lease," the Ricardos stomp all over the floor all day to make the Mertzes miserable.

• Prior to the "Lucy Fakes Illness" episode, the Ricardos' twin beds were pushed together. They had separate sheets and bedspreads, but they essentially had a king-sized bed. Two episodes later, in "Breaking the Lease," the beds are together again, and they remain that way until the pregnancy episodes.

• In "The Ballet," Fred first mentions his vaudeville act, Mertz and Kurtz. At that time his partner's name was Ted Kurtz. It later changed to Barney.

• In "Fred and Ethel Fight," Ethel goes home "to mother," but she doesn't say where that is, nor is her mother ever mentioned before or after this episode.

• In "The Moustache" episode, Ethel claims her talents are musical comedy, singing, dancing, acting, and voices. Fred's are tap dancing, soft shoe, smart quips, and vaudeville.

• In "Pioneer Women," it is mentioned that the Ricardos have been married for ten years, and that Lucy had a Swedish grandmother.

• Ricky calls breakfast pancakes "tortillas," "flap cakes," and "hot jacks" in "The Kleptomaniac." Lucy calls them "hot cakes."

• Lucy gives her address as 623 East 68th Street when she orders meat in "The Freezer." She also tells us that steak is $1.89 a pound. Also in this episode we learn about Ethel's Uncle Oscar and Aunt Emmie.

• Lucy wears the same outfit in back-to-back episodes, "The Freezer" and "Lucy Does a TV Commercial."

• In "Lucy Does a TV Commercial," Ricky mentions "Mr. Hatch." Wilbur Hatch was the musical director of the Desi Arnaz Orchestra on the *I Love Lucy* show.

"LUCY HIRES AN ENGLISH TUTOR"

"THE INDIAN SHOW"

"THE INDIAN SHOW"

"RICKY'S HAWAIIAN VACATION"

"Lucy Has Her Eyes Examined"

"BONUS BUCKS"

"MR. AND MRS. TV SHOW"

• In "The Anniversary Present" we learn that Lucy's wedding ring cost $50, and that Ricky used to eat rice for breakfast in Cuba.

• Lucy has ticklish feet—we find that out in "The Handcuffs."

• In "The Anniversary Present," the Ricardos give the Mertzes a gift (which Ricky later breaks) of a 20" TV set. What would they think of the modern 60" flat-screen variety that comes in color and high definition digital, and hangs on the wall?

• In "Redecorating," we first hear about "party lines." Party lines (or shared service lines) are telephone lines that are shared between homes. They were less expensive than single party lines, and often the only option available. In the Mertzes' apartment building, nosey neighbors were able to listen in on private conversations, but conversely it was a good way to spread the word in case of emergency or danger.

• Lucille Ball became pregnant during the end of season one of *I Love Lucy*. They had to move the scheduled filming up to the summer in order to end in November so she could rest before the baby's impending arrival in January. In "Redecorating," Lucy wears loose overalls to disguise her expanding waistline, and in "The Black Eye" she wears a stylish maternity jacket for the first time.

• Fred claims to have played at the Palace Theatre in Jamestown in 1927, a reference to Lucy's hometown. The Palace Theatre opened there in 1923 and was billed as a "high-class vodvil (vaudeville) house." It was later renamed the Reg Lenna Civic Center after the Lenna family made a large donation toward its renovation.

"MERTZ AND KURTZ"

"LUCY GETS IN PICTURES"

"CHARM SCHOOL"

• In "The Club Election" one of the club members is named Lillian Appleby after one of Lucille Ball's teachers. Her name was changed to Carolyn in later episodes. Also in this episode, the names Pauline Lopus and Marion Strong, both childhood friends of Lucy, are mentioned.

• In "The Black Eye," everyone ends up with a shiner. The guys get their right eyes blackened, while for the gals it's the left that takes the hit.

• Poor Ethel had a total of three coincidental middle names. She was Ethel Roberta (Roberta was Vivian's middle name), she was Ethel Mae (Mae was Vivian's mother's middle name) and she was Ethel Louise (Louise was the middle name of Bill Frawley's former wife). She may have been confused, but at least she kept it all in the family!

• *I Love Lucy* was the first TV show to have a Hispanic actor, director, or producer.

• *I Love Lucy* was the first TV show to be filmed on a converted movie soundstage in front of a live audience.

• Lucy Ricardo was the first visibly pregnant actress on TV, and the birth of Little Ricky was the first time the issue of pregnancy and childbirth were discussed on TV.

• Almost all the celebrity guest stars were men.

• Desi Arnaz, Jr. never appeared on *I Love Lucy* as Little Ricky. He did appear in the very last episode as a little boy in the crowd. Lucie Arnaz never appeared on *I Love Lucy*, but both children had roles in *The Lucy Show* and were co-stars on *Here's Lucy*.

• Each *I Love Lucy* audience consisted of three hundred people. They sat on grandstand bleachers erected by the Safeway Steel Scaffolding Company.

• Desi Arnaz usually memorized his lines in one reading.

• Out of the four *I Love Lucy* stars, Lucille Ball was the only one who did not graduate from high school.

•Ethel and Fred Mertz were named after an Indianapolis couple that had been neighbors of Madelyn Pugh.

• Ricky Ricardo's was the only birthday never mentioned on *I Love Lucy*. Lucy's ("Lucy's Last Birthday"), Ethel's ("Ethel's Birthday"), and Little Ricky's ("Lucy Gets Homesick in Italy" and "Lucy and Superman") were all celebrated. Even Fred's was discussed ("Too Many Crooks"), but no one ever remembered poor Ricky!

• Episode 26 ("The Marriage License"), which aired April 7, 1952 was the first TV show to be viewed in 10,000 U.S. homes.

• The bread used for the episode "Pioneer Women" was rye, because it stayed fresher longer than white bread. After the episode taped, the bread was cut up and distributed among

"LUCY MEETS THE QUEEN"

"DON JUAN IS SHELVED"

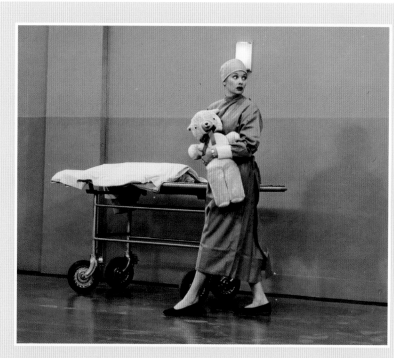

"NURSERY SCHOOL"

"Lucy Meets Orson Welles"

"Little Ricky's School Pageant"

"Return Home from Europe"

cast and crew.

• Reverend Clifton Moore, Rabbi Alfred Wolfe and Monsignor Joseph Devlin were chosen to read the "pregnancy" scripts in order to filter out any objectionable material about the impending birth. None of them ever changed a word of the scripts.

• Desilu Productions received just more than two hundred letters disapproving of the Ricardo pregnancy. However, Lucille and Desi received more than thirty thousand congratulatory notes after their son was born.

• When Lucy was trying to decide how to get out to California, she said she wanted to go by bus or car so Little Ricky could see the country. However, Little Ricky ends up staying behind and flying out later with his grandmother, so Lucy's reason for taking the slow boat didn't pan out.

• The schedule Ricky put Lucy on in "Lucy's Schedule" includes time set aside for showering, dressing, breakfast, washing dishes, making beds, cleaning, laundry, fixing nails, marketing, lunch, phone calls, taking a nap, doing her hair, watching TV, cooking dinner, and dressing for bed. At least he included everything!

• Ethel and Miss Lewis have clothes made from the same fabric. Ethel wears a dress in episode "New Neighbors" which, while it doesn't match the style of Miss Lewis' dress, was cut from the same cloth.

• Lucy and Ethel wore matching outfits in "Job Switching," "Lucy and Ethel Buy the Same Dress," and "Mertz and Kurtz."

• In "The Séance," Fred's fez says TEHRAN (the capital of Iran).

• In "The Adagio," Lucy grabs her stomach. It had been less than four months since daughter Lucie had been born by caesarian surgery.

• In "Cuban Pals," Lucy claims both her parents had red hair, which is strange since she has to use henna rinse!

• Lucy's Kramer's Kandy Kitchen uniform has a belt but Ethel's doesn't.

• American radio host Mary Margaret McBride is alluded to twice, once when Fred calls Ricky "Ricky Margaret McBride" ("Job Switching") and once when Ethel calls herself "Mary Margaret McMertz" ("The Million-Dollar Idea").

• Miss Lewis is seen only once, but she is mentioned in "The Courtroom" as the baker of Ethel and Fred's anniversary cake.

"Lucy Gets Chummy with the Neighbors"

Jockey Johnny Longden and wife with Desi and his mother Dolores on the set of "Lucy and the Loving Cup"

Lucy and the Borden Twins, who memorably appeared in "Tennessee Bound"

• In "The Club Election," the recent conventions that aired on TV are mentioned. As this episode was written in early fall of 1952, the writers must have been alluding to the 1952 presidential conventions. The Republican Party nominated Dwight David Eisenhower and Richard Millhouse Nixon, while the Democrats chose Adlai Stevenson and John Sparkman.

• In "Ricky Has Labor Pains," Ricky's doctor lights up a cigarette! You'd think the American Medical Association would have let him know they're bad for his health.

• When Ricky brings home a hot fudge sundae and sardines for a pregnant Lucy, the sardines were real (they couldn't find anything that looked enough like sardines to fool the audience), and Lucille really ate them!

• "The Spider" is the "ewwwww" sound made by Lucille Ball in dozens of *I Love Lucy* episodes. It was named that by her radio writers because she had to make commercials for Jell-O and she felt awkward doing them, so Jess Oppenheimer rewrote them as nursery rhymes, and Lucy would play characters such as Goldilocks and Little Miss Muffet. When the spider would "sit down beside her," she would change her voice and make that sound, so it became known as her "spider" noise. In "The Ricardos Change Apartments," there is a triple "spider" when Lucy, Ethel, *and* Fred all do it at the same time!

• In "California, Here We Come!" Mrs. McGillicuddy wants Ricky to bring her manuscript to Dore Schary, but in the episode "Don Juan is Shelved," she doesn't know who the MGM mogul is.

• In "Lucy Wants New Furniture," Ethel claims to never have made a dress, but if Fred only lets her buy one a year, you have to wonder where she gets the others!

•Don't try this at home! Lucy attempts to cut an electrical wire with scissors in "Ricky and Fred Are TV Fans," but if she did that in real life, she would have electrocuted herself!

• When the women's club is going around the room describing their show business experience in "Lucy and Ethel Buy the Same Dress," Ethel, who probably has more know-how than anyone, doesn't mention all her years in the biz.

• In "Redecorating the Mertzes' Apartment," the gang talks about color choice (Fred's is orange) but they never tell us what the final color is. We also learn Fred and Ethel have lived in the apartment for twenty years.

LUCY AND LITTLE RICKY (KEITH THIBODEAUX)

KEITH THIBODEAUX

• Actress Alice Wills plays Madame X in "Too Many Crooks," and even though she is caught, we never see her face.

• Ethel asks Lucy if she can borrow her 1920s hat ("Lucy Gets Her Eyes Examined"), but according to Lucy, she would have only been a baby during that decade. Maybe she inherited it from Mother.

• In "Ricky's Old Girlfriend," Lucy claims to have gone to "junior college."

• We learn that Lucy has an Aunt Martha in "The Million-Dollar Idea." Interestingly, Ethel has an Aunt Martha, too.

• Actor Frank Nelson played several show-host roles on *I Love Lucy* including Freddie Fillmore ("The Quiz Show" and "Lucy Gets Ricky on Radio") and Dickie Davis ("The Million-Dollar Idea"). He was also the train conductor in "The Great Train Robbery."

• Lucy claims she's been to Hollywood in "Home Movies."

• In "Bonus Bucks," Ricky claims there are eight million people living in New York City. In that same episode, Lucy and Ricky spend $54 on cabs, and get a $50 speeding ticket.

• Poor Ethel, she must be so confused. Sometimes she can

"THE TOUR"

223

play the piano ("Breaking the Lease" and "The Operetta"), but other times ("Lucy's Club Dance" and "Ragtime Band") she is all thumbs.

• Fred Mertz goes to bed at 10PM ("The Black Wig").

• In "The Sublease," we learn that Lucy was twenty-two when she married Ricky.

• Fred has to borrow 15¢ to ride the subway in 1954.

• In "First Stop" the train rattles by the cabin four times before the gang decides to hit the road.

• The Texas Ann Motel in Amarillo, Texas features air conditioning, phones, TVs, and radios in the rooms. It's three hours from Ethel's hometown of Albuquerque.

• Fred and Ethel accompany the Ricardos to Hollywood and have their own room (317) in the hotel for months. Fred said he wouldn't pay to go on the trip, so who paid their hotel bill?

• In "Don Juan and the Starlets" Lucy said she met Ricky when Marion Strong asked her to go on a date with a Cuban drummer.

• The phone number at MGM is Texas 0-3311.

• Fred and Ethel's anniversary is May 3rd ("Hollywood Anniversary").

• Before they start selling raffle tickets, Lucy and Ethel find $82.50 around the house in couches, sugar bowls, and piggie banks. Too bad they need $3,000 to book their European trip.

• In "The Passports" we learn that Lucy was born in 1921. Lucille Ball was actually born in 1911.

• In "The Passports," Lucy and Fred fall asleep on the ferry and have to rush to the passport office to get their papers signed; Lucy arrives half asleep and has trouble taking her oath and signing her papers. Fred unplugs the wall clock so the officer doesn't realize the office should be closed, but strangely enough we never see Fred take his oath.

• The gang spends five days crossing the Atlantic aboard the *S.S. Constitution*. On the ship they read the *Sun Lane News*.

• In "Paris at Last," Fred collects some Christmas cards at the American Express office, but not a word is said about the holiday, or anyone missing spending it at home. Lucy and Ricky don't even mention Little Ricky or Santa Claus!

"TENNESSEE ERNIE HANGS ON"

"THE MILLION-DOLLAR IDEA"

• In their Florence hotel room, Lucy and Ricky have to climb the staircase five times while they wait to speak to their son on the phone in the lobby.

• Ricky, Ethel, and Fred are in movies in Hollywood (not to mention the bottoms of Lucy's shoes), and Ethel is in a movie in Rome, but no one ever speaks about seeing them.

• No one should feel bad about paying for luggage on a plane these days, because in 1955 they apparently charged $50 to take a cheese onboard!

• Lucy ruins at least seven pizzas when she works at Martinelli's pizzeria.

• Has Fred been hanging around Ricky too long? In "Deep-Sea Fishing" it's Fred who mutters, "Ai yi yi yi yi!"

• While marooned on a desert island in Florida, Ricky and Fred come across actor Claude Akins, and Ricky says he was in a movie with Claude in Hollywood.

• Ricky's Uncle Alberto smokes Corona Grande cigars. In later life, Desi Arnaz owned a horse-breeding farm called Corona.

• For Christmas one year Little Ricky got a train set, a bicycle, a drum kit, a robot, and a toy monkey!

• When jockey Johnny Longden appeared on *I Love Lucy*, he was awarded a trophy (well, sort of) for having earned 4,961 victories in his career. When he retired in 1959 he had earned 6,032, including the Kentucky Derby, the Preakness, and Belmont about Count Fleet in 1943 (earning him the Triple Crown). He still holds several track records at Santa Anita Park.

• In 1956 it cost $3.08 to take the train from New York City to Westport. Sixty years later, it costs about $11.00.

• In "Building a Barbecue," they finally deduce that Lucy's ring fell on a tray, which makes sense, but then how did it

"RETURN HOME FROM EUROPE"

get imbedded into a hamburger? Even if it fell on top of a hamburger someone would have seen it before they put it on the grill.

• In "The Golf Game" Lucy is the first to drive the ball because her hand is second from the top. Later on, when she and Ethel play with Jimmy Demaret, he goes first because his hand is fourth from the top.

• In "Lucy Fakes Illness," they talk about the hind legs of a bird, but a bird only has two legs!

• In "Vacation from Marriage" the Mertzes claim to be married for twenty-two years. In the very next episode ("The Courtroom") they are suddenly celebrating their twenty-fifth wedding anniversary.

• In "The Saxophone," Lucy plays "Glowworm" for the first time. She later claims to only know how to play "Sweet Sue" on the sax.

• In "The Black Eye," Fred purchases roses and gladiolas to send to Lucy on Ricky's behalf, but only the roses make it into the box.

• In "Lucy Learns to Drive," watch as Ricky has to step over the cable that connects the Cadillac and the Pontiac

• In "Lucy's Show Biz Swan Song," watch as Lucy turns during her dance—she pulls the string holding up her bloomers so they fall down around her ankles when the dance ends.

• In "Lucy is Jealous of Girl Singer," Ricky steps on Rosemary's dress on purpose so it will rip.

• In "Ricky Loses His Voice," Marco Rizo, Desi Arnaz's piano player, portrays himself on the show. In this episode he mistakenly called Ricky Ricardo, "Des"—as in Desi Arnaz.

• In "Lucy Changes Her Mind," Lucy is seen reading a magazine, and what's on the cover but *I Love Lucy*!

• In "Lucy Goes to the Hospital," Fred purposely unlocks Lucy's suitcase so the clothes will spill out.

• In "Ricky's Hawaiian Vacation," Freddie Fillmore talks about Ethel's mother but calls her Mother Mertz, instead of Mother Potter.

"LUCY FAKES ILLNESS"

I'm Home!

On December 10, 1951, Ricky Ricardo first uttered the words that he would become famous for saying—"Lucy, I'm home!" At the very end of the second season, his 'spression morphed into the more generic, "Honey, I'm home" and since then it has been heard on modern TV shows such as *Full House*, *The Fresh Prince of Bel Air*, *Gilmore Girls*, and even British sitcoms such as *After You've Gone*. *Hi Honey, I'm Home* was even the title of a sitcom that aired on ABC and Nick-at-Nite in the early 1990s (Gale Gordon as Theodore J. Mooney [from *Here's Lucy*] was the show's first guest star).

"Lucy, I'm home!" can be found in:

"The Fur Coat"

"Lucy Fakes Illness"

"The Moustache"

"The Saxophone"

"No Children Allowed"

"The Ricardos Change Apartments"

"Honey, I'm home!" can be found in:

"Never Do Business with Friends"

"Lucy and Ethel Buy the Same Dress"

"Changing the Boys' Wardrobe"

"The Business Manager"

"The Fashion Show"

"In Palm Springs"

"Ricky's European Booking"

"Ragtime Band"

The Games People Play

In the 1950s, television had just been invented, and many Americans didn't have one in their homes. The radio was a very popular form of entertainment, for music and ball games. Many families and friends also gathered to play games, and the *I Love Lucy* gang was no exception. Lucy and Ethel often got together for a friendly game of cards with their frenemies, and there were many nights that the foursome got together to play bridge or gin rummy. Here is a list of some "old fashioned" games and pastimes that were enjoyed by the Ricardos, the Mertzes, and their friends:

Baseball	Gin	Old maid
Basketball	Golf	Ping pong
Boxing	Hearts	Poker
Bridge	Hot and cold	Scrabble
Canasta	Kite flying	Shuffle board
Charades	Leap frog	Solitaire
Crossword puzzles	Mah jong	Word finds
Fishing	Mother may I?	

LUCY GREETS FANS IN A BREAK
FROM FILMING "IN PALM SPRINGS"

Fandemonium

The cast of *I Love Lucy* always understood that the show was a success in large part because of the loyalty of its fans. Fans of the show wrote letters, sent telegrams and gifts, visited the set, sat in the audience during tapings, and even stopped by the Arnaz home in Beverly Hills and knocked on the front door!

Sixty years later *I Love Lucy* fans are still going strong. They get together to watch DVDs and laugh. They take trips to the Lucille Ball-Desi Arnaz Center in Jamestown, New York, and to the Lucy Tribute in Orlando, Florida. They go on *I Love Lucy* cruises, and visit chat rooms, websites, and blogs

to write about their favorite moments. Students write term papers and present reports on the show and its actors. Books are published. Fans dress as their favorite characters for Halloween. Some folks even throw Lucy-themed birthday bashes and bat mitzvahs. Unlike so many forgotten shows of its generation, *I Love Lucy* continues to bring people together across the globe and in dozens of languages.

If you ask the average person who "Lucy" is, you will be told about the wacky redhead who was always trying to get into show business. You will hear how watching the show helped that person through a divorce, a move, or an illness,

and always made him or her feel less alone in the world. You will hear how hard he laughs when Lucy stuffs chocolate in her mouth, or how she tears up when Lucy tells Ricky they are going to have a baby. You can't get away from the good feelings the show and its characters have to offer, especially in a world that is often frightening and uncertain. We know that Ricky will always love Lucy no matter what; that Ethel will always help Lucy out of whatever jam she gets herself into, and that Ricky and Fred will be pals again at the end of the day.

Relatives and strangers, the famous and the unknown love *I Love Lucy*. It's universal; it crosses gender and age differences, and social and education divides. It is the quintessential "feel good" comfort show; it's the mac and cheese of TV. Here, a few folks tell you why they love *I Love Lucy*:

....

"I love *I Love Lucy* because it paid for my college education."

—Katharine Desirée Luckinbill, granddaughter of Lucy and Desi

....

"I love Lucy because she had moxy, style, and grace. She and Desi discovered how to connect with people on multiple levels and they had a very positive and progressive message. To me, their message was a human message that read: Be happy, laugh a lot, love a lot, give a lot, and you'll do just fine. I have always respected and loved them for that."

—Joe Luckinbill, grandson of Lucy and Desi

....

"I love *Lucy* because it reminds me of the importance of the healing power of laughter, and how much we all crave a source of unconditional love."

—Lucie Arnaz

....

"Thanks Mom and Dad…for keeping the planet a happier place for sixty years. We need your love and laughter now, more than ever."

—Love, Desi and Amy Arnaz

LUCIE ARNAZ

"I love *I Love Lucy* because it gave me the opportunity for a long and happy association with Lucille Ball and her family. *I Love Lucy* was over when I started working for Lucy, but Desi Arnaz was still very much in the picture. The couple shared children who were close to their father—he was still working on the Desilu Studio lot and Lucy relied on him for good advice until he died. He was also the most charming person I ever met.

"Working for Lucy was the job of a lifetime, and I still consider it a big part of my life as I'm close to Lucie and Desi, Jr., and involved with the Lucy-Desi Center in Jamestown, New York. I met wonderful and exciting people through all the years and stay in touch with many of them. Being in a position to hear inside stories of *I Love Lucy* behind the scenes from friends like Cleo Smith (Lucy's cousin) is really fun, to say the least. Lucy always had the best crew—many were with her through all the series years, and some are still close to me, which makes me happy. I continue to be grateful to Lucy for the best job anyone could have."

—With love, Wanda Clark, secretary to Lucille Ball from 1963 to 1989

AMY AND DESI ARNAZ

"I love *Lucy* because *it* and *she* make people smile. Without hesitation, a person's first response when recalling or being reminded of the show (or of Lucy) is to smile. Lucy makes the world a better place. What would be a better tribute to your life than knowing that you made the world smile?

"My formative youth years happened when Steve Martin was a young comic. He played the banjo and had a bit that said something like 'The banjo is such a happy instrument. You can't play a sad song on the banjo . . . it always comes out so cheerful.' That's Lucy. Think of Lucy, and the show, and no matter what else is happening you will smile."

—Ed Dudley, Senior VP of Sales and Marketing, Rocky Mountain Chocolate Factory (home of Lucy's Chocolate Factory)

"I love Lucy because she keeps me connected to my mother—then, now, and always. I first started watching when I was little. My mom would turn it on and then leave me to watch while she did her chores. I learned and memorized the episodes and could always tell you what was going to happen next. As my sisters grew we would watch together, and we would then play together. I would always be Lucy and my two sisters would take turns being Ethel or sometimes one of my sisters would be Carolyn Appleby. I always wanted Ricky to be my husband; I had a huge crush on him! My mom would join us in watching and we would just laugh and have a great time together.

"When my nephew and nieces were born my mother did the same exact thing—sit them in the family room

and put *Lucy* on, thus beginning a new generation of *Lucy* lovers. My mother is no longer with us, but we still all get together in her honor and arrange *Lucy* marathons. Now Lucy, Desi, William, and Vivian are all with my mother in heaven and I am sure they watch us from above and smile.

"So thank you, Lucy and friends, for giving me a memory of my mother that will be cherished as long as I live!"

—Donna Piumetti

"Lucy was part of the American family. She is part of the world family. And I was fortunate enough to be a part of her family. I first met Lucy when I was a twelve-year-old fan. She wanted to make sure I was going to be more than just a 'fan.' She wanted to make sure I was going to stay in school and get a job. Once I was gainfully employed, she came to visit me at the department store where I was working, and she bought a whole bunch of things from me. After that date, Lucy invited me to her home—not just as a fan, but as a friend. If I ever had a problem at home she

MICHAEL STERN AND LUCY

MICHAEL STERN AND DESI

would always ask me, 'Did you talk to your parents?' Lucy would always put me on the right track. I love Lucy because of the Lucy I knew. She was the love in *Lucy*!"

—Michael Stern, "Lucy's Official #1 Fan"

"It is difficult to put into words why I love *I Love Lucy* since it has been a part of my life for so long. In fact, I can't remember *not* being a Lucy fan, so it is like writing about a long-time family friend or relative. I suspect this is the case for countless people around the globe.

Lucille Ball, Desi Arnaz, Vivian Vance, and William

Frawley, in the characters they brought to life in *I Love Lucy*, have not only entertained generations of people, but they have become fixtures in our lives—always there and always available to provide a pick-me-up in times of frustration, sadness, or even when just feeling a bit 'dauncy.' They have certainly helped me along the way. The stars, along with Jess Oppenheimer, Madelyn Pugh Davis, and Bob Carroll, Jr., Bob Schiller, and Bob Weiskopf have left a priceless legacy to the world and I can't thank them enough.

But one of the great things about *I Love Lucy*'s legacy, and the legacies of Ball, Arnaz, Vance, and Frawley, is that it is not simply consigned to just DVDs and VHS tapes ready to play at a moment's notice; it has grown to a flourishing and ever-expanding community bringing together people from all walks of life that wouldn't otherwise have the opportunity to interact.

One only has to look at the festivals that have been so successful in Jamestown as well as the festivals in Burbank to see this phenomenon in action. Whether we are clamouring for an opportunity to meet with such legends as William Asher and Dann Cahn, who are integral parts of this living legacy, or having an opportunity to speak to people like Lucy's brother, the late Fred Ball, or their cousin Cleo Smith; seeing the places and things that influenced the life and career of Lucille Ball; and even going on souvenir hunts, we are all united in our celebration of this legacy. One of the greatest pleasures is seeing the same people at these events year after year, with new faces (those who are newly minted Lucy fans or long-time fans who have only just learned of "the watering hole") thrown into the mix. Through these events—and through vibrant online communities—I have met some of my closest friends; that's one more thing for which I am indebted to the 'original Fab Four.'

I also have *I Love Lucy* to thank for introducing me to so many wonderful actors that I might not have otherwise been exposed to. Preserving and promoting the legacy of Gale Gordon has become a particular interest of mine, as well as celebrating the life and work of everyone who dropped into the "Lucy" world, including the criminally underrated Mary Jane Croft, Mary Wickes, Charles Lane, Doris Singleton, Shirley Mitchell, Frank Nelson, and everyone from the biggest guest stars, like William Holden and Van Johnson, all the way through cameo queen Hazel

Pierce. (If any woman has performed more 'walk-bys' in television history than Hazel Pierce, I'd like to hear her name!) Their connection with the immortal *I Love Lucy* has ensured that new generations are introduced to their work in perpetuity. That's yet another phenomenon stemming from the now ubiquitous rerun that began with a visit to 623 East 68th Street.

It could also be argued that another significant part of the *I Love Lucy* legacy is its use as a teaching tool. Where else could one learn about the days when they used to race little girls at Churchill Downs? *I Love Lucy* contains some great tips for cramming for those last-minute history, geography, English, and math exams. For example:

History/Geography

• Columbus discovered Ohio in 1776.

• Marie Antoinette was guillotined to scrape the barnacles off her hull.

• Kildoonan, Scotland may or may not be located between Gillespie and Babalu.

• Locarno and Lucerne are *not* the same place.

• A trip to the Mayo Clinic does *not* translate to 'a lovely trip to Minnesota.'

• Despite what you may have heard, there is no such place as West Jamestown.

Economics

• The more you spend the more you save.

• Naming your next child (or re-naming your current child) is a perfectly valid part of the barter system.

Law

• It is illegal to read someone else's postcard (until after they're postmarked; then they're fair game).

• When coming up with a worthy cause for your raffle make sure you have a good, phony name.

• If you find the name of a rum company on your marriage licence, get panicky.

- Anyone with the last name O'Brien is *never* above suspicion.

. . . .

Home Economics

. . . .

- The size of yeast cakes *does* make a difference.

- When serving rice, a pound per person will do in a pinch.

- No good can come from pinching chocolates to see what kind they are.

- In case of fire, is it best to save family photos or your henna rinse? The answer may surprise you.

Civics

- There's never a *wrong* time to caucus.

- The sap runs every two years.

- In election season, always make sure you're courting the right Knickerbocker.

- You'll go farther with Ethel.

Joking aside, Lucy, Desi, Viv, Bill, every single writer, crew member, guest-star, and bit player have left an incredible legacy. It has always been there for me when I've needed it. I would also like to thank Lucie Arnaz and Desi Arnaz, Jr., for sharing their parents' legacy so generously and ensuring it is preserved for generations to come. As 'Lucy' fans we have been very lucky—and dare I say spoiled—this regard. It is very much appreciated."

From Brock Weir, administrator, The Lucy Lounge (http://www.gale-gordon.com/lucylounge):

DIANE VINCENT AS LUCY

"I love *I Love Lucy* because—oh, for all the obvious reasons. Because after sixty years it is still the best comedy on television and because at times there's nothing I would rather watch. Because it continues to make me laugh out loud, even though I've heard those brilliantly written and delivered lines a million times over.

Now for the less obvious—but more personal—reasons. I love *I Love Lucy* because since 1995 I have been blessed to make my living as a Lucy Ricardo impersonator. She has afforded me wonderful opportunities to travel and do festivals and represent her character at Universal Studios Hollywood. She has enabled me to work alongside Desilu alumni and some of Lucille Ball's closest friends and family, whom I have come to know and love. I honed much of my seemingly natural comedic sensibilities by watching her on *I Love Lucy*. Playing Lucy Ricardo has made me a better performer. Both watching and portraying her have given me a richer life. So I am deeply honored and grateful to remain one of a privileged few who can proudly say I Love Lucy because I 'live' Lucy!"

— Diane Vincent, actress

"Soon after Carole and I first met, we often talked about our memories of watching all of the *I Love Lucy* shows in the '50s, during the time when we were both finding our ways to careers in the acting profession.

What was so special about Lucy, Desi, and the other extraordinary actors who made that show so brilliant? From an acting point of view, we both agreed that it was this simple fact: When watching the show, you *believed* everything the characters said! You believed they were who they said they were! That they could do and say those outrageously funny things, and be completely believable and honest while saying and doing them, and could make you howl with laughter while watching it! They were never 'acting!' They all made it seem like it was happening for the first time, and believing that everything they said was the truth! That is what great acting is all about! To this day, Carole and I continue to aspire for that result whenever we perform! And now, watching reruns, we continue to love the truth in what Lucy, Desi, Viv, and Bill were so graciously giving everyone who was watching!"

—Carole Cook and Tom Troupe, actors and dear friends of the Arnaz family

CAROLE COOK

"I would never describe myself by saying I am *I Love Lucy's* biggest fan, because many people believe themselves to be the 'biggest, greatest, most devoted, most loyal' fans of Lucille Ball and *I Love Lucy*. I have heard these words uttered by thousands of visitors during the fifteen years I worked for and was associated with the Lucy-Desi Museum in Jamestown, New York.

I was in the unique situation of being a Lucy fan that got to experience other Lucy fans and their love for the show on a regular basis. From the woman who kissed the floor upon entering the museum because she had arrived at her Mecca, to the numerous tour groups enjoying *I Love Lucy* trivia questions, rarely did I see anyone come through the door with a sour face. And on the rare occasion that a grumpy look was seen entering, that frown would be replaced by a broad smile, as they would exit. . . . I love *I Love Lucy* because I have witnessed its power firsthand: its power to change how a person is feeling, to brighten someone's bad day, to lift the spirits of the sick and elderly, and to provide laughter that is timeless and appeals to all ages. It is this power to heal the human spirit that makes me just ONE of *I Love Lucy's* biggest fans."

—John Schillner, Jamestown, New York

....

"Every Monday night, at 8PM Central time, I was armed and ready with three chocolate chip cookies and a cold glass of milk waiting for *I Love Lucy* to come on.

There were times when Lucy and Ethel were planning their schemes and I would think to myself, 'I don't think this is going to work' as I put my hand over my eyes and watched the TV through a little crack between my fingers.

Example: when the girls were having so much fun and thinking how easy it was wrapping the candy in the chocolate factory. That is, until 'that woman' (their supervisor) yelled, 'let her roll' and then, 'speed it up a little!' And also with the commercial Lucy attempted for Vitametavegamin, the vitamin syrup that had started out tasting soooo bad was starting to taste sooo good . . . and, well, you know the rest. I guess you could say that all the predicaments Lucy and Ethel got themselves into made me laugh so hard my sides hurt.

I Love Lucy brought me to a world that was so believable, I could see it happening. We continually watched her go from . . 'oh I can do this,' to, 'oh no!' It was a ride from fun and fantasy to consequences, but each time the show ended you were always left with a smile on your face, and a laugh in your belly, until the next time you heard Lucy say, 'oh Ricky.'"

—Bruce Bronn, Unforgettable Licensing

....

"Desi Arnaz was one of the most significant figures in American entertainment, but not in the way most people realize. His gifts as a bandleader and as a proponent of Latin music at a time when that sound wasn't so familiar to the American public were obvious, but his great, even extraordinary, contributions to Hollywood were more subtle than that.

We all know that Lucille Ball was the great female comic genius of the twentieth century, and that their show, *I Love Lucy*, which in my opinion is the most important television show ever produced, was a perfect showcase for her tremendous talent. What we don't often appreciate is that Desi was the man who understood her talent and knew exactly how to spotlight it; if *I Love Lucy* made history, it is especially because of Desi's genius as a producer. The television we watch to this day is based on a format he created to help his wife be her very best. The three cameras, the filming instead of going live in New York, the studio audience, the concept of reruns—all of it shot Lucy into the stratosphere. All of it shaped the next sixty years of television production. Practically all of it was his idea. All of it exploded a system that even the studios hadn't fully appreciated, but he did.

All of it born from this Cuban man, being so totally Cuban that he sang songs in Spanish every week on national television (another subtle breakthrough with huge impact: say thank you, Gloria Estefan and Shakira), this Cuban man who was told that people wouldn't buy him with an American wife (never mind they'd been married for years), this Cuban man invented the sitcom form as we know it. And all of it stemmed from the love of one man for one woman, putting the very truth to his statement that *I Love Lucy* was never just a title. Aren't we lucky that it happened? And aren't we lucky that it was true?"

—Raul Esparza, actor

"I love *I Love Lucy* simply because it is timeless, believable, and absolutely hysterical. . . . Do I know the shows, line by line, and what happens in each episode? Unashamedly, the answer is yes. Is it considered fan worship? After nearly fifty years of continuous viewing, the answer is yes! *I Love Lucy* possesses the extremely rare combination of superior writing and credible acting, which keeps the show fresh. In my mind the four characters actually lived and breathed.

. . . I am very pleased to say that I have had the pleasure of meeting several people directly involved with *I Love Lucy*, including the Redhead herself. I am sincerely grateful for what they have created and left for the world to enjoy. My life has certainly been richer for it."

—Rick Carl, advertising art director

"There are countless reasons I love *I Love Lucy*—the clever, finely crafted storylines, the memorable character actors, the unique and essential contributions of Desi Arnaz, Vivian Vance, and William Frawley and, of course, the glorious comedic talent of Lucille Ball. But to me, the show's key appeal has to be in its reflection of the genuine real-life love between Lucy and Desi that's so palpable on the screen. Still today, after decades of seeing the episodes over and over, I remain fascinated to watch the interaction between the two: the physical nuances, the knowing glances, the occasional tender moment; it is a love that is as timeless as it is real. I believe the authenticity of that relationship is the secret ingredient that imbues the show and its characters with a credibility that make the often outrageous plots believable. It is by no mere marketing coup that the heart symbol and the word 'love' are indelibly associated with a series that couldn't have been more aptly named."

—Tom Gilbert, journalist and co-author of *Desilu: The Story of Lucille Ball and Desi Arnaz*

"I love *I Love Lucy* because it gives the lie to Thomas Wolfe's adage that 'you can't go home again.' Sure you can! I do it every time I turn on the show! Every time I hear the theme song begin, I am transported back sixty years to where I first saw the program—in my parents home, with all of us gathered around the set.

Yes, I am a 'first generation' *Lucy* fan. I saw the Ricardos and Mertzes in first-run prime time, every Monday night on CBS. There were six of us in those days—mom and dad and four kids. Everyone had his own favorite shows—everything from *Howdy Doody* to *Mister Wizard*, from *Milton Berle* to *Boston Blackie*. But on Monday nights, we all watched *Lucy*.

The series, moreover, has proven to be one of my life's few constants. Other elements have come and gone. I have lived many places, done many things—but *Lucy* has always been there. The show has never failed to entertain, to brighten my day, to leave a smile on my face and a warm glow in my heart."

—Thomas Watson, author/DVD producer

"*I Love Lucy* is a quilt of comfort; colorful, familiar, secure. Experiencing the humor gifted to us creates the warmth of being tucked in and kissed goodnight as our smiling souls drift into the world of comedy. Thank you to Lucie and Desi for sharing your 'larger than life' parents with all of us. I know that this was a sacrifice; however, the laughter has been a healing Band-Aid that made the pain of illness and loss far more tolerable. Oh, blessed laughter!"

—Patricia Polson Lowe, Ridgefield, Connecticut

"As a child actress I always stopped to watch *I Love Lucy*. Thus began my love of comedy. My birthday is the day after Lucille Ball's birthday (different year) and they used to play *I Love Lucy* marathons the weekend of her birthday here in Los Angeles. In between each show they would say, 'Happy Birthday!', And as a child I made believe they were doing it all for me.

This show is Comedy 101. I've had no greater teacher than watching Lucille Ball's timing, reacting, pantomime, expressions, light bulb moments—say a thousand words with only a quick movement of her eyes. No university or school can teach you that. Then the other three principles followed suit, Desi Arnaz, Vivian Vance, and William Frawley—all playing comedy volleyball with Lucy and never dropping the 'Ball,' but rather enhancing the comedy game with many points (laughs) with their own individual genius. The writing was clever and simple.

They didn't need to resort to sexual references, toilet humor, vulgarity, controversy or anything complicated—only good clean everyday situations Americans could and still do relate to. They were the first to do shows about getting a job, gossiping, spying on your neighbor, wanting something maybe you weren't suppose to have or want, good intentions with not-so-easy results, and on and on and on. All of which have been depicted since over a million times in situation comedies but never as well or as perfectly as the inventors and the cast of *I Love Lucy*. I thank them for blazing the trail and making me fall in love with the art of comedy."

—Suzanne LaRusch, star of the one-woman theatrical
   presentation *An Evening with Lucille Ball: Thank You For Asking*
   (www.AnEveningWithLucilleBall.com)

Tom Watson

"It's not the writing—I didn't appreciate the writing at the time. It wasn't the comic timing—I was too young to know what that meant. It wasn't the three-camera technique, or even the excitement of the live audience. There are many

Suzanne LaRusch

people who have written books on all these things; who have explained in detail what made that show go down in television history. For me, it was more than all that. It was personal. *I Love Lucy* was personal to me. I understood the people. They were people I could've known. They had fights, they made up. They yelled, they hugged. They laughed, they cried. So did I. They were real.

Of course there was chemistry, comedic timing, and musical ability, but at the time, I didn't care or appreciate any of that. I just knew that's who I wanted to be. It's how I wanted to live my life. To grow up, but never lose the ability to be playful and childlike. To never take myself too seriously. To marry a man (though he may yell a lot) who I knew would love me until his dying day. The older I get I see just how important these things are. As Desi Arnaz wrote, 'I Love Lucy was never just a title.' To me, *I Love Lucy* was never just a TV show."

—Cathy Anastasi, Altoona, Pennsylvania

"Genius comes in many forms and is responsible for many important contributions to the world and to our quality of life. Comedy is often overlooked and undervalued, and yet where would we be as a society if we did not laugh?

A little girl from Jamestown, New York grew up to become the undisputed Queen of Comedy. Her impact was immediate and immense, and has continued to ripple to this day. She was a genius, she is an icon, she is a legend! Her contribution of laughter to the world will be remembered in every piece of chocolate we eat, and each out-of-tune note we hear. She gave us so much, and so to her I say, 'thank you, and I love *I Love Lucy.*'"

—Miles G., Jamaica, New York

"When Lucille Ball stepped onto the set as Lucy Ricardo, she set the stage for millions of individuals facing troubles in life. For a half hour, she made the strife of life vanish, and shared a sliver of her comedic genius to the world."

—Natalie T., Pennsylvania

"I love *I Love Lucy* because I grew up watching her with my grandparents who have since passed away. They were my best friends and I miss them every day. When my husband and I had a baby girl, the first and only choice of name for her was Lucy!"

—Christa K., Akron, Ohio

"My mom was watching *I Love Lucy* when she went into labor, pregnant with me! Lucille Ball has always made us both laugh."

—Lucy M., Munroe Falls, Ohio

Licensed Products

Long before there were *Happy Days* dolls, Hulk Hogan action figures, and Big Bird books, *I Love Lucy* was among the first television programs to produce licensed products. Desilu recognized early on that fans of the show were interested in buying products associated with the show. When Lucy became pregnant in real life and on TV, the product marketing exploded. There were items for the nursery, such as cribs, changing tables, baby baths, diaper bags, and hobbyhorses. There were Lucy and Little Ricky dolls and toy furniture for little girls. Moreover, there were *I Love Lucy* bedroom and living room furniture sets. There was even linoleum and paint for the home.

In terms of fashions, you could choose from *I Love Lucy* pajamas, aprons, dresses, blouses, sweaters, robes, and costume jewelry. For entertainment there were comic, coloring, and paper doll books, games, record albums, sheet music, and conga drums. Philip Morris even put out a little booklet called *Lucy's Notebook* which contained recipes and party hints, not to mention coupons for Philip Morris products. At one point people were referring to Desi Arnaz, Jr. as the "The 50 Million Dollar Baby" because of the merchandising interest in him, or, more accurately, his alter ego, Little Ricky Ricardo. Lucy and Desi refused to exploit their son in connection with the products, although pictures of Desi, Jr. and his mother did appear on the very first *TV Guide* (April 3, 1953). All of the merchandise surrounding the *I Love Lucy* baby was related to Little Ricky Ricardo, not Desi Arnaz, Jr.

When the show ended, the merchandising transferred over to Lucille Ball, since she continued to star in television shows of her own. There were more comic books, board games, and children's mystery novels. In the later 1980s, Lucille Ball was once again approached with merchandising ideas, this time harkening back to the *I Love Lucy* years,

with a series of collector plates and porcelain dolls. Several of these were produced before her death in 1989.

After her death, her family formed Desilu, too, in an effort to manage the estates of Lucy and Desi. Since then, hundreds of products including calendars, dolls, books, mugs, cookie jars, DVDs, luggage, costumes, ice cream, chocolate, T-shirts, and umbrellas, have been manufactured. Even sixty years after the show's debut, it seems that admirers still cannot get enough of the Ricardos and Mertzes. In fact, many diehard fans have entire rooms of their homes designated to the gang and their adventures. They say they like to go to their special "Lucy" rooms for comfort and laughs. How wonderful that a show six decades old can still bring so much joy to so many.

Extra, Extra, Read All About It!

A Book, by Desi Arnaz, 1976.

Desilu: The Story of Lucille Ball and Desi Arnaz, by Coyne Steven Sanders and Tom Gilbert, 1993.

The Fifties, by David Halberstam, 1993.

For the Love of Lucy: The Complete Guide for Collectors and Fans, by Ric B. Wyman, 1995.

I Had a Ball: My Fanship with Lucille Ball, by Michael Stern, 2011.

The I Love Lucy Book, by Bart Andrews, 1976.

I Love Lucy (audio book), by Susan Doll, 2009.

I Love Lucy: Celebrating 50 Years of Love and Laughter, by Elisabeth Edwards, 2001.

Lucy at the Movies, by Cindy De La Hoz, 2007.

I Love Lucy: The Classic Moments, by Tom Watson, 1999.

I Love Lucy Paper Dolls, by Allan Glaser and Rick Carl, 2004.

Laughing with Lucy: My Life with America's Leading Lady of Comedy, by Madelyn Pugh Davis with Bob Carroll, Jr., 2005.

Love, Lucy, by Lucille Ball, 1996.

Loving Lucy, by Bart Andrews and Tom Watson, 1980.

Lucille Ball: The Life of Lucille Ball, by Kathleen Brady, 1994.

Lucy A to Z: The Lucille Ball Encyclopedia, by Michael Karol, 2001.

Meet the Mertzes, by Rob Edelman and Audrey Kupferberg, 1999.

Mr. and Mrs. Cugat, by Isabel Scott Rorick, 1937.

The Other Side of Ethel Mertz, by Frank Castelluccio and Alvini Walker, 1998.

The Quotable I Love Lucy, by Tom Watson, 2001.

Something from the Oven: Reinventing Dinner in 1950s America, by Laura Shapiro, 2004.

Diamond Jubilee Products

MATTEL'S 60TH ANNIVERSARY LUCY AND RICKY DOLL SET, COMMEMORATING EPISODE FOUR, "THE DIET"

THE ASHTON DRAKE GALLERIES VITAMEATAVEGAMIN DOLL

AMERICAN GREETINGS LUCY AND RICKY 60TH ANNIVERSARY CHRISTMAS ORNAMENT

MOUNTED MEMORIES FOR THE DIAMOND JUBILEE

LUCY AND RICKY CHRISTMAS ORNAMENT

MEAD 2011 *I LOVE LUCY* ANNIVERSARY CALENDAR

Index

250

Thank You

A book this size is never the work of one person. There are so many who helped and guided and listened, that it's impossible to thank them all. I hope they all know who they are.

To the children of Lucille Ball and Desi Arnaz, Lucie and Desi; their spouses, Amy Arnaz and Larry Luckinbill; and their children, Simon, Joe, and Kate Luckinbill (Phyllis loves ya, baby!), and Julia and Haley Arnaz. And to Aunt Cleo Smith and Aunt Zo Ball for all their love. Thank you all, my darling friends, for the love, support, and trust you have given me for all these many years. I could never thank you enough, so I won't even try.

To my husband, John Moscone, my rock, for his unending support and encouragement; to our son, Andrew, who is my hero; to my parents, Penny and Don Edwards, for all they taught me; to my in-laws, Barbara and John Moscone, for their love and acceptance; and to my sister, Susan Edwards, for putting up with me (and for not snoring when we shared a room).

To Greg Jones and everyone at Perseus Books, and especially to Cindy De La Hoz, my editor and friend, and to Melissa Gerber, my designer.

To Bruce Bronn, Mark Shachtman, and Brian Eich at Unforgettable Enterprises, my champions and my friends.

To my beloved godson, Blake, with love from his "Auntie Abay." And to his mother, Susan, my lifelong sister.

To Nancy and John Alexanderson, and Scott and Whitney, who rescued me when I needed it most.

To my aunt Janie Reeve for her loyalty and love.

To Beth Aaronson, Holly Bergeron, Holly Dunn, Robin Keller, Judy Nachowitz, Lori Peterson, Alison Sedney, Julie Schechter, Mary Smith, Betsy Weber, Liz Wendell, and Trudi Yeager—the ladies of the club—for their support, friendship, and laughter.

To Kieth Dodge, whose wise teaching, counsel, and friendship continues to influence me from above.

To Tana Sibilio, who keeps me in stitches and in sandwiches.

To all the members of the Chancel Choir First Congregational Church, Ridgefield, who make my soul sing every week.

To Tom Watson, Michael Stern, Wanda Clark, Frank Gorey, Keith and Kathy Thibodeaux, Richard Brock, Rick Carl, Gregg Oppenheimer, and all the fans who inhabit this sometimes crazy but always wonderful world of Lucy and Desi and all their pals.

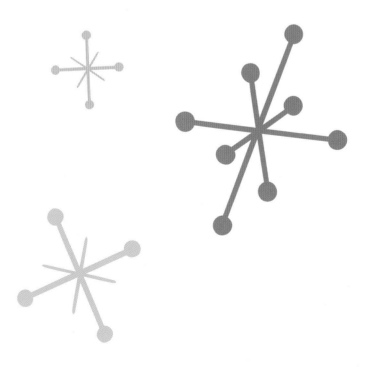